Praise {

Courting: A Ten

"The journey of a senior tennis player is indeed a rich tapestry of experiences, both on and off the court. The mental fortitude required to stay competitive over the years is immense, and it's fascinating how this book captures the essence of that struggle. It's not just about the game; it's about the life lessons learned, the social dynamics navigated, and the personal growth that occurs in tandem with one's athletic pursuits. Such narratives not only inspire but also provide a deep insight into the human spirit intertwined with the sport."
– Steve Duffel, president, National Men's Tennis Association

"*Courting* is a fast-moving, inspirational book which chronicles Bill's tennis journey. He beautifully weaves his love of tennis competition with his personal ups and downs, his concern for society, and his love of family and friends. His writings are a true testament to the fact that 'tennis is a sport for life.'"
– Brenda Carter, winner of 7 International Tennis Federation world senior individual championships and more than 60 USTA senior national championships

"Bill's journey and return to tennis epitomizes the fact that there is more to wellness than just exercising. In balancing physical activity, social interactions, and a clear purpose, Bill's courting of tennis shows us the importance of finding something we love and pursuing it – regardless of age."
– Tom Woolrich, wellness coordinator, Glenaire, a Life Plan Community

Courting

A Tennis Memoir

William R. Finger

atmosphere press

"Having put his racket down when he was a boy, he had remembered everything. His body had remembered... A clean hit can stop time. Sometimes it can feel like the only peace there is."

- Cheta Maroo, *Western Lane* (Farrar, Straus and Giroux, 2023)

"In my mind, an amateur is one who competes in a sport for the joy of playing, for the companionship it affords, for health-giving exercise, and for relaxation from more serious matters.... [H]e accepts cheerfully all adverse breaks, is considerate of his opponent, plays the game fairly and squarely in accordance with its rules, maintains self-control, and strives to do his best, not in order to win but rather as a test of his own skill and ability.... The returns which amateur sport will bring to those who play it in this spirit are greater than those any money can possibly buy."

- Richard S. Tufts, on a plaque at the entrance to Pinehurst Country Club, Pinehurst, North Carolina

Table of Contents

Part IV

Part I

1

Crossing a Threshold

I hold Veronica's hand tightly as she toddles along, almost 11 months old. Behind the tall fence to my left, I steal a glance at the little kids on the last tennis court in a row of six. They swing little "sawed-off" rackets at squishy balls that bounce about half as high as regular tennis balls. They aim over a short portable net placed on one side of the regular court.

The tug at my hand pulls my attention back to the little bundle of humanity who is squatting to pick up a rock. Veronica, my first grandchild, seems to notice every tiny stone along the sidewalk as we meander toward the Millbrook Tennis Center clubhouse. I watch her turn the pebble over in her hand but intervene as she moves it toward her mouth. She gives it to me after only a minor pull of her hand. We inch forward.

"Swing up on the ball to get the topspin," a male instructor is saying. I look up and see my daughter, Veronica's mother, guiding her racket upwards on her forehand stroke. The thud of the ball against the strings brings a smile to my face.

Dana's class is ending now, and she comes up to us on the sidewalk. "Hi baby," she says to her little one. As mother and daughter connect, I look up at an accomplished junior player hitting well-grooved topspin strokes on a nearby court. I can see myself at his age, more than 60 years ago, when I started hitting forehands on the Millsaps College courts in

Jackson, Mississippi. I swung with my arm horizontal to the ground, a flat shot with little spin. As the style of instruction has changed, so has the racket, from sticks of wood to fiberglass compositions. Despite these evolutions, the same rectangular court frames opponents in a battle of will and skill, psychology and physicality, fun and diversion.

Dana's set of tennis classes ends as the winter holiday season approaches. When my wife, Georgia, and I decorate our Christmas tree, she hands me the small pewter tennis racket. For maybe 35 years now, I have hung this ornament, which looks like it could hit a solid volley. Spring comes, the miniature racket is stored with the other ornaments. Again, I walk along the edge of the courts with little Veronica, now 15 months old, as Dana resumes tennis classes. Echoes of balls on the strings ring a bit louder in my ears, maybe to neglected sections of my heart.

In May, I turn 70.

The thud of balls across the Millbrook courts takes me back to my early years in Raleigh, right after Georgia and I got married. The Millbrook courts were my home base throughout my 30s, where I met players and competed in tournaments. The director ran the events under a tent borrowed from a funeral home, with card tables and handwritten draw sheets. In my office today, a silver goblet sits next to a jar of pennies, reminding me of those years. The engraving reads: "RPRD [Raleigh Parks and Recreation Department], Mens Singles Winner, 1979."

Threshold, Inner Voice

A month after my 70th birthday, Georgia and I fly to Boston, the first stop on a vacation, where we meet her high school friend, Betsy, and her husband, John. They take us to their 200-year-old stone house, once a water-powered mill, south of the city. Inside, rackets, tennis shoes, and cans of balls are spread about on floors and shelves.

That evening, during a lovely dinner, John asks, "Do you still play?" On an earlier visit, John took me out to his local tennis club where we found that we played at about the same level.

"Not much," I say. "But I can usually hit fine, even if I haven't played in a while."

"Do you want to play tomorrow?"

"That sounds great, but I have only grooved walking shoes for our trip. They won't work on the red clay."

"I'm sure we can find you something. Georgia and Betsy will have plenty to talk about while we play. It's a plan!"

After dinner, we move into the adjacent living room where stacks of John's paintings lay against the walls. We relax in the cozy old furniture that fits a converted mill house. Commanding equal space to his large canvases, or at least equal to my attention, are piles of sneakers and rackets John pulls into the center of the room.

"I think I can find something for you to use here," he says, looking up with his wry smile and then down at my feet. "What size do you wear?"

Examining the shoes, all about a size too small, I pick the Stan Smith golds, well-worn with cracks in the side, hoping they provide more width for expansion. I slide them on, painfully, my toes crunched. Then I pick up various racket choices and settle for one with all the strings intact and a nice spring to the hand.

The next day, a beautiful June morning, John Baker guides his old Volvo along a narrow drive through the woods. We are the second car in the small make-shift parking area, next to a set of five red clay courts that date from the 1900s. We chat and stretch, two old warriors in our 70s out for another go at it. I haven't played serious tennis for decades, only an occasional doubles game, maybe once a year.

I squeeze my feet into undersized shoes, take up a stray stick of graphite, bounce the heel of my hand against a trampoline of woven nylon, and go out on a lovely little playground of clay for an hour of decent forehands and backhands. Beneath tall pines in rural Massachusetts, I relax on the clay court. This casual hit-around seems a bit like sitting in meditation, the spirit of the breath flowing through the torque of my torso as it unleashes power into the stroke.

"You had a kind of serenity out there today," John says as we gather our towels. "It is amazing you can hit that well with so little practice."

"And I saw again your seriousness about the game," I say. "Working with your equipment to compensate for your elbow problem. So steady coming out so many times a week. Your game shows all of the practice."

"Yes, but I lack some of that serenity," he says. John learned his leftie strokes as a child with instruction in New York's Central Park and found a lifelong groove as a teenager in a tennis-centered summer camp in Sturbridge, Massachusetts. He was filling holes in his family life through the rigors of tennis. For me, tennis offered an escape from the pressures and hypocrisy of religion and race in Jackson, Mississippi. For both of us, a tennis court was a place of refuge, of peace.

As we head back to the old water mill, to this haven for art and rackets and reflection, I wonder about combining this serenity and seriousness. At age 70, perhaps the time has come to return to my old spiritual home.

"Aging becomes a time for visiting the temple of your memory and integrating your life," wrote the Irish poet John O'Donohue. "Integration is a vital part of coming home to yourself. Old age can be a wonderful time to develop the art of inner harvesting."

Do I feel the same spiritual call to the sounds and swats at the ball? Is it time to enter this sanctuary once again? Am I too old to jump back into this vigorous game?

"We find ourselves crossing some new threshold we had never anticipated," wrote O'Donohue. Listen "with complete attention until you hear the inner voice calling you forward."

Re-Joining the Tennis World

The next day my wife and I board a cruise ship in Boston. We head up the coast and then down the St. Lawrence River. After several nights in Montreal, at the end of the cruise, we go to a modest condo outside of Quebec. Several mornings, we watch Wimbledon matches on television before we head out sightseeing. My tennis memories mingle with the commentators' discussions of shot choices, strategies, nerves, and fitness. The urge to play serious tennis grows stronger.

After our Canada trip I look at the prices of three tennis clubs in Raleigh, along with potential partners, clinics, and locations. By far the best fit is the Raleigh Racquet Club or RRC, where I have played occasionally over the years as a guest.

Monday, August 7, 2017: I park in the long, narrow lot next to the clubhouse. Inside, a young man stringing a racket directs me to the business office upstairs. I pay the $450 joining fee and get a brief tour of the facility: small restaurant, four permanent indoor courts, locker rooms, a small gym, and a large lounge area. Outside, a patio looks out over a stadium court. Two rows of six green composition courts are down a hill to the left. Above the stadium court to the right are two other groups of six courts.

I take a deep breath. I have joined a tennis club for the first time in my life. I have standing to reserve courts, to take lessons, to be on club teams. I text the news to my old friend, Dick Heidgerd, a long-time member of the Raleigh Racquet Club: "Money paid – member!"

Dick and I met on the Millbrook courts in our early 30s

and played in North Carolina-based tournaments for a few years. He started playing as a kid and says tennis was a lifesaver during a bout with depression in his first year of law school. Tennis became an integral part of his life.

After some success with Dick in the 35-and-over division, I retired from serious tennis. Over the last three decades, I accepted an occasional invitation from Dick for a doubles match at the club but never had the time or inclination for sustained, serious tennis.

Wednesday, August 9: Dick asks me to join his regular doubles game, but all regulars show up unexpectedly. Instead, I play singles with another extra, losing the first set to this young, hard-hitting guy with big topspin strokes. But I am not embarrassing myself, and find a bit of my old magic, even taking a 5-2 lead in the second set. But I begin to gasp for more wind between points and have to stop. My normal exercise in a casual senior cardio class at a fitness center has not prepared me for serious tennis.

Thursday, August 17: I get a text from Dick asking if I can substitute for him in a doubles match. Tennis at the Racquet Club, complete with multiple doubles matches and many friends, is a way of life for Dick and his family.

Then a new text arrives: "You are a mythical creature to my RRC friends. I have bragged about you so much, so play like a pro! But don't choke. Make me look good."

After the match, I report back to Dick. "Mythical is sadly gone to the ordinary – missed returns, double faults, flubbed volleys. I had fun and remembered how hard doubles is. You have to AIM where you hit."

• 2 •

Finding My Footing

Like many players in their 60s and 70s, Dick now plays in team tennis leagues rather than traditional stand-alone tournaments. He lobbies me to join his Racquet Club men's doubles team for those 65 years and over. I appreciate Dick's informal sponsorship of me to his buddies. I feel more at home in this crowded field of new faces and more confident that I can play good tennis as well. The team captain is glad to add me to the roster.

The team plays eight matches, once a week through the fall. Each match consists of three separate doubles contests. The main competition is a Millbrook Tennis Center team.

Our first match is September 14 on our home courts. The captain puts me in the number 1 flight, paired with 6 feet 2 inches Mike Rhaney. More than 50 years ago, Rhaney was one of the first African Americans recruited to attend an all-white high school in Tallahassee, Florida. Now a successful IT consultant and active in administration at the Racquet Club, he seems at home in this mostly white world of tennis players. The match starts at 6 p.m., still bright in daylight savings time.

We both hit good volleys and overheads, winning without too much of a struggle. Another Racquet Club team wins, giving us a 2-1 victory for the match. The teams share beer and conversation on the deck overlooking the row of courts.

Many guys on both teams have known each other for years. All are new acquaintances to me. Joining a few conversations, I feel welcomed but not connected. From the deck I look out at my best friend – the tennis court – and the promise it holds at this stage of life.

The next Thursday we play at Millbrook, where I walked with Veronica only months earlier. Some guys, including my partner from last week, Mike Rhaney, do not play on hardcourts, which Millbrook has, because they are too jarring on old knees. The soft green clay at the Racquet Club is much easier on aging joints. Several years before returning to tennis, arthroscopic surgeries in both my knees removed a torn meniscus, which took care of pain. My knees have felt fine since.

At the hardcourt match, I play with one of Dick's good friends, another lawyer named John Mitchell. Again, I hit good volleys and overheads and have only one double fault. I am amazed that I can perform so well in serious doubles matches two weeks in a row after my decades-long layoff from competition. After the match, Mitchell calls Heidgerd to report that I played great, especially for a 3.5 player. Dick then talks to me. "Finger, you've got to scale things back," he says laughing. "You don't want to be too good a 3.5."

Each doubles team in this "7.5 league" must have one person rated 3.5; the other is usually a 4.0 (i.e., 3.5 + 4.0 = 7.5). These numbers are from the United States Tennis Association (USTA) National Tennis Rating Program or NTRP, which did not exist when I stopped playing tournaments at age 40. To get a rating, a new player must do a self-rating process on the USTA website. As an ex-college player, I am probably a 4.0 or maybe a 4.5 player after I get back my old game. But after decades off, a 3.5 rating seems fair for now. Dick and the team captain encourage me to rate myself as a 3.5, which makes the team stronger because I can be paired with a 4.0 player.

In early October, several weeks after our match at

Millbrook, I play with John Mitchell again on the hard courts. Our opponents win the toss and choose to serve first. They hold serve to lead 1-0. As we change sides, John says, "You serve first. You hit 'em well last time over here." I step back to the service line with confidence but with a service motion that is not yet well grooved after my long layoff. First point, double fault, love-15. Still, the game is young. Second point, another. Now, at love-30, we're in a hole.

"Come on, Bill. Just get the first one in," Mitchell says, in an encouraging tone.

Third point, same thing. By now I have lost all confidence, along with any muscle memory in a good serve. I met my partner only three weeks earlier, a colleague who is fast losing confidence in me as well. I finally get a serve into play and we win the point. Now, serving at 15-40, I serve my fourth double fault of the game. Our opponents do not have to hit a single ball in the court to win; I give away the four points they need.

Embarrassed and angry, I apologize to Mitchell, who seems a bit speechless. While we are only behind 2-0, my confidence is sliding fast. He must be thinking that he cannot rely on me to lead the way to a win. I just made one of the worst errors in all of tennis, giving a game away without making your opponent hit even a single ball. I try to steady myself and find my strokes, but I cannot call up my body memory, which hit so many good shots decades earlier and even a week ago. As the match goes on, I hit easy serve returns and volleys into the net. Mitchell and I each hit some good balls, winning enough games to make our losing score presentable. The Racquet Club team wins only one of the other two matches, so we lose the overall contest, 1-2.

As I drive home from Millbrook, without hanging around to drink a beer, I think about the double faults. *Maybe if I had just hit a few serves in that game, we could have been 1-1 at the start. We might have won our match, and then the Racquet Club team would have won 2-1.* In sports, second guessing what might have happened is futile, if not inevitable. I am frustrated and angry at myself for the double faults and other errors, for letting my team down. Gradually, about halfway through the 25-minute ride home, my frustration settles down. As a bit of calm returns, I ask myself: *How important are those errors, really? I have a new second grandchild. My body is holding up to hard tennis. I hit four double faults in one game, so what? I am not the first person to do that, and I will not be the last. No one lost a job or any money. No one got hurt. And I have matches ahead to think about.*

By the time I pull into my driveway, my mind is more questioning than blaming. I accept my double faults as part of the process of returning to tennis. No one expects me to be as good as I was decades ago, the mythical player Dick Heidgerd has told his friends about. But I do not know how good I am or might become. I can improve gradually and acclimate my game to the strategies of this crafty senior crowd, practice hitting drop shots and lobs along with strokes. And I need to practice my serve. I can accept myself as I am now, a work in progress. Winning is not everything, but losing sure makes acceptance of myself harder.

Our captain sends around the match summary from the Millbrook defeat but gracefully leaves out my double fault fiasco. I need to tell Dick, since he functions like my informal sponsor among his long-time buddies at the Racquet Club. Still embarrassed, I wait two days before calling. Then, before I can start talking, Dick jumps in.

"Well, congratulations, you are in fact a 3.5." He is chuckling, not scolding. "I told Ayden [a member of the team] that you would win every time this fall. He said, 'No he won't.' He was right."

I'm smiling now. "Your buddy John called and told you, right?"

"Yeah, he did," Dick says laughing. "But it'll be OK. You'll keep hitting good shots. Don't worry."

The next Thursday night, just a week after our loss at Millbrook,

I play again on the soft Racquet Club courts with big Mike Rhaney with his bad knees. Back in the tennis saddle, to mix sports metaphors, I hit well in my third time out with Rhaney, and we win again. But the Racquet Club team loses the overall match, as well as outings the next two weeks. Millbrook wins the fall season, with the automatic bid to the state tournament in November. But because the Racquet Club won the state championship last year in this division, we get invited to the tournament too.

Singles

While I am enjoying the weekly doubles matches, I also want to revive my singles game. A perk for new members of the Racquet Club was a free singles lesson. Dick thought I would get to hit with the head pro, who is national champion in the 35-and-over division, an exciting prospect. Instead, as I approach the pro shop front desk at my appointed time, I see a stocky man who is African American.

"Hi, I'm Malik," he says. "I understand you're new to the club." I nod. "We're going to the upper courts to hit."

"Great," I say, hiding my disappointment in getting someone other than the top pro. We chat a little walking up past the stadium court to the oldest group of courts. I ask about his background.

"I grew up playing on public courts, then kept playing in the Army," he says.

"Oh, I grew up on public courts too."

"Then I got a coaching job at Mount Olive University and eventually came here." Sounds like he got hooked on the game and worked his way up to a teaching job at a premier tennis club. I like his spunk, including how he made his way into a career not historically friendly to African Americans. As we begin to hit, I also see that he can hit well and knows his tennis.

I do not know what to expect from the lesson. While I played a lot of tennis over the decades, I never had personal instruction. My high school coach was a journalism teacher, and my college team was guided by an assistant football coach near retirement.

Malik takes me through the basic shots: forehands, backhands, volleys, serves. After about 30 minutes, we take a break and talk. "You hit a very flat ball," he says. "You hit it well, but you might do better in the long run to add some topspin." I nod, remembering the topspin shots from my first opponent at the club, one of Dick's friends. When we go back out, I do manage to swing up and over the ball on my forehand, adding a little topspin. I get more net clearance, adding safety for shots, and try to have the shot land at least behind the service line. Adjusting my backhand is much harder.

Malik comes up to the net and shows me how to rotate my grip slightly to the left and how to swing up on the ball, following through toward the sky. I have always swung my backhand either flat or sliced, with my arm extending parallel to the ground. After the grip shift, I hit the ball into the bottom of the net. "Swing up on the ball," Malik reminds me. "And follow through much higher."

He hits more balls as I try again and again. Finally, when I focus on following through up to the sky, which feels awkward, a few topspin backhands sail a foot or more above the net and drop into the court well behind the service line. "That was great," Malik says. "You can get it. You'll just have to work at it."

As we walk back, I ask what he thinks my rating should be. "At least a 4.0," he says. "Maybe a little higher." After the lesson I wonder if I should adjust my game to include topspin options. First, I need to find some guys to play and see how my singles game unfolds.

On a September Wednesday at 2 p.m., the club is nearly deserted. A mother is taking a private lesson on the upper courts. Her son is hitting with a friend on the stadium court, below the large clubhouse patio. The pro shop is quiet, no tugs on the racket stringing machine. A few teenagers are working on computers in the lounge, home-schooled kids waiting for the tennis academy to start the afternoon workout. Two white-haired women in dresses sit on the patio discussing bridge strategy.

A muscular, middle-aged man arrives with a bag filled with rackets. "Hi, I'm Marshall," he says. "I guess you're Bill." We head down the hill to the lower bank of six courts. I got Marshall's name off the board outside the men's locker room, where members looking for games put contact information, along with NTRP rating and preferred times to play.

Most of the guys playing in the doubles matches do not play singles; a few do but are still working, making daytime games difficult. Marshall has flexible hours with a big computer backup firm; he likes to play during the day so he can pick up his seven-year-old son from school and be home for the family evening routine.

"I'm back from New York and want to work on my game after a week off," Marshall says as we reach the court, pull our rackets out, and start warming up. He shares a bit of his tennis journey. "I started playing seriously in my late 30s. I've tried to model my game after Nadal, hitting big topspin strokes."

While we hit different types of strokes, we are at about the same level. At age 70, I give up about 25 years in quickness, but I am more consistent and can generally match his power.

I take a 5-2 lead, but his big topspin shots begin to find the mark. The high bounces give me trouble. Also, even though I am quick for my age, I cannot reach some of the sharp angles he hits near the sidelines. He ties it up at 6-6 and wins the seven-point tiebreaker, taking the set 7-6. After playing an hour and 15 minutes, we quit for the day with him leading 2-1 in the second set. He must pick up his son. I'm exhausted and glad to stop.

"Strokes and fitness – both need work," I write in my tennis notebook that night.

Five days later, Marshall and I play again, this time at 10:45 in the morning, which suits us both. I play better, have more endurance, but still get tired. I have too many double faults but manage to split sets with him 4-6, 6-4. Coming back to win the second set is satisfying.

"Singles takes a lot of mental and physical energy," I write in my journal that Monday night, and add: "My back hurts. My left foot hurts. My wrist and thumb hurt a lot warming up. I managed two full sets but could not have played a third." Singles matches in tournaments are two out of three sets. I need to get in much better shape before I can manage that.

Doubles Team in State Tournament

On Thursday, November 9, the group text messages start at 6:29 a.m. from the 65-and-over team captain. "Eight am matches are on schedule," he says. We know the rain forecast looks bleak, but if the USTA official in charge says to take the court, we have to be ready. About 900 people are registered for the USTA end-of-year NC team tennis state championship. Matches are being held across 14 locations in the greater Wilmington, NC, area. "We need you here for the 9:30 match," the next text says.

I am about two and a half hours from the site of my match. My 6 a.m. alarm has just gone off. I should have plenty of time. The tennis center at the Pine Valley Country Club is nestled off the main highway that runs past the University of North Carolina at Wilmington and on to Carolina Beach. I find our captain at 9:10. "Glad you made it," he says. "I don't know how much you'll get to play though."

A light drizzle is starting, and very dark clouds are overhead. Even so, we are heading to the court soon. I stretch, run in place a little, and get my head into gear for a tournament match. Tall Mike Rahney with his bad knees, a familiar face in a sea of tennis players, greets me. We win the toss and snag the first game on our serve, just as a light drizzle gets harder. The deluge arrives before we can start another game.

I was planning to play Thursday and Friday, sharing a room with my friend Dick Heidgerd at the Hampton Inn, headquarters for the event. Others can play only on Friday and Saturday. A few plan to stay Thursday through Sunday. But now the rain has the schedule in limbo. Players still wet from racing off courts stream into the large Hampton Inn lobby. I find Dick and head to his room to get into casual clothes for what looks like a day without tennis.

One of the large conference rooms off the lobby is packed with vendors selling every kind of tennis-related paraphernalia. The crowds spill into the sprawling lobby with side seating areas. People are playing cards, talking tennis strategy, catching up with friends from around the state, and sitting quietly with a book or a coffee. The circus-like atmosphere is both invigorating and intimidating. I have not seen so many tennis players together in a long time, probably since a trip to the U.S. Open in New York many years ago. But I'm not sure where to plug in. My team members are spread out in the area, some staying with wives in a cottage, others in motels. I look at some of the pricey vendor merchandise and then settle into a corner chair to wait for teammates and a plan for this rainy day.

The rain washes out all Thursday matches after 9:30 in the morning. The USTA officials are working out make-up times for the missed matches. I will play, as planned, in the match scheduled for 9 a.m. on Friday. We will learn in the morning if the courts are playable that early after the torrents of rain. Texts start coming in regarding dinner arrangements now, not match start-times.

Thirteen guys spread down a long single table at a seafood restaurant that night. I know the names of most of them but have only played with two or three. Some of the men, including me, play on both the Racquet Club 55-and-over and 65-and-over teams. The two captains juggle the lineups, based on the tournament schedule, travel plans, and successful duos from the season. The food is delicious, the conversation far-reaching, including whether we will play in the morning.

The next morning, the captain's message is a thumbs-up, get to the courts. Our match is scheduled at a gated community called Landfall. The tennis center is nestled within the sprawling high-end complex of million-dollar homes, some backing up to a bay with large boats docked ready for deep-sea fishing. We get through the gates and check in with the officials assigned to that site. They say that we have a one-hour delay, as the courts finish drying, with matches starting at 10.

Greg Cooper, one of the team captains, is my partner today. A friendly corporate executive still working in his late 60s, Greg played at a small college years ago. He serves first. On two points, when the opponents hit weak returns, I move quickly across to Greg's side of the court to cut off the shot with a winning volley, a "poach" in tennis jargon. I poach throughout the match, and we hold Greg's serve regularly. I have three double faults in one of my service games, which we lose, and I miss some easy volleys. But generally, I play well, and we pull out a close win, 6-4, 7-5.

After the ritual handshake at the net, I turn to walk toward the stylish gazebo-like area to get my tennis bag. One of our opponents comes up to me and says, "Which one of you is the 3.5?" He has an edge in his voice.

"I am," I say, hoping that will end the questioning.

"Did you play in college?"

"Yeah, a long time ago. I stopped playing tennis about 30 years ago and just started back this fall."

My explanation does not slow him. "Ex-college players are not 3.5 players," he mumbles a bit as he turns away. I hope his complaining is nothing more than a disappointed loser, not something more serious, like a protest that I should be rated as a 4.0 player.

I turn to my gear and start putting my racket away. The conversation seems to be over. Greg has overheard the exchange. "Don't worry about it," Greg says. "You registered correctly as a 3.5 player. That's where you were after such a long layoff. We're fine."

Late that afternoon, I play a match with a new partner in the 55-and-over division. We lose 6-2, 7-5. Both of our opponents are stronger players than I am, and I cannot tell which one is the 3.5 player. Any concerns I have about being rated incorrectly are lost now as I review the match in my head. While I hit some good shots, my serve returns were not consistent enough and cost us some points. Still, for my first match with the younger age group and a new partner from the Racquet Club, I feel O.K.

Nearly dark now on Friday, my tournament experience seems to be over for the year. I don't think I can return to Wilmington for a Sunday match if our team reaches the final. The two-hour drive back to Raleigh gives me plenty of time to reflect on this end of my new tennis season.

I am sorting out friendships, schedules, strategies, and my old strokes. I have been playing tennis for more than 60 years now, and I feel like I have returned home. But so much is new. New people, new age brackets, new team structures and rating systems, new partnerships, and new skills needed. I feel like I am starting a new job. My task in this job is to figure out what I need from tennis at this stage of life and how to go about getting those needs met.

Maybe I also need to remember and embrace the nature of tennis itself, as the writer and tennis aficionado David Foster Wallace framed it. "I submit that tennis is the most beautiful sport there is," Wallace wrote in a long *Esquire* story. "It requires body control, hand-eye coordination, quickness, flat-out speed, endurance, and that strange mix of caution and abandon we call courage."

Courage: that is what I need for this new stage of life and a new commitment to serious tennis.

● 3 ●

Intense Workout

In the 60 years since I first swung a tennis racket, I can never remember playing before the sun rose. When I turn into the Raleigh Racquet Club parking lot at 6:45 a.m. on December 12, 2017, the clubhouse is dark. Another driver pulls up just as I am wondering whether to wait or go knock on the door. He looks confident as he lifts his double-wide tennis bag onto his shoulders, like the backpack size the pros use. We introduce ourselves in the dark.

"I'll check the back door first," Bo says. Locked. Then he heads around the corner of the clubhouse to the main door that opens onto the patio overlooking the stadium court. "Success," he calls.

I pick up my single-wide Babolat bag with the separate compartments for my two rackets and other stuff like towels, sweat bands, and balls. (The Babolat brand of tennis gear is new to me.) For a few weeks now, I have been enjoying carrying this single bag instead of the rackets in one arm and a gym-style workout bag in the other. Inside, I move down the stairs to the "Court House," a permanent structure with four indoor clay courts adjoining the main clubhouse. I know my way to these courts, where I have been playing in a regular Thursday night doubles game during the first months of the winter season. I am looking for the "Intense Workout" clinic that starts at 7 a.m.

Three guys are already working hard on court 4, all at the net, two on one side and one alone, with a pro encouraging them and feeding them balls. They stretch hard for low volleys, grunting and bouncing on their toes, as if in a tough tournament match. These guys are way above my play level and much younger. I wonder how I can manage this rotation. Another pro solves that mystery, heading toward Bo and me with two rolling grocery cart-like baskets of balls. As I take off my sweatpants and a sweatshirt, another player, also named Bill, joins us. Then a fourth person, a woman named Jill.

My body feels strong as I start the first exercise, hitting volleys and short strokes from the service line, which is about half-way between the net and the baseline. Philip, the young pro leading the clinic, feeds us balls from across the net. I start on the left side of the court, the "ad" side, hitting backhands and volleys. The other Bill is on the deuce side to the right. After we each hit 10 balls, Philip pauses just enough for Bo and Jill to move in. Philip moves the drill quickly, so we never relax. The other Bill and I switch sides as we rotate behind the other two. Just as I catch my breath, our turn comes for another 10 balls each.

In the next drill we move back to the baseline, again 10 balls each and swapping sides of the court in each rotation. Finally, we get a break, just as I am feeling my cereal, reminding me not to eat much before this clinic again. I take deep breaths as we all gather up the hundreds of balls we have hit by now, filling the large baskets with the little yellowish spheres.

Then we begin hitting volleys and overheads, alternating, up for a volley, then back-up for the overhead. The intensity increases. As I finish the second 10 balls, I have to lean over to catch my breath. "Keep walking around," Bo says. "Your lungs are more open that way and you can get more air than leaning over." I try it and feel better.

I picked this cardio workout as my first clinic to try at the club. Playing regularly in the fall improved my stamina, but

I know I need more endurance, especially for singles. Today, now maybe 7:25 in the morning, I am chasing down lob after lob and trying to smash overheads, which takes an explosion of focused energy. As I walk about, catching my breath, I am proud of how far I have come.

In the next exercise, each of us takes a turn hitting 20 balls. We stay on the court for as long as we get a racket on the ball. Philip hits it away from us, running us back and forth. In my first round, I feel my will sagging, reaching the balls but with weak strokes.

"Come on Bill, you can make it." I hear the others in the class cheering me on. And it helps. I find another burst of energy to reach my last few balls and hit the 20. But I can barely finish the second set of 20. The others are gathering up balls again as I sit at the bench to catch my breath. "Take your time," Bo says.

Sitting, breathing as deep as I can, watching these people I have just met gather up the balls, and supporting me, feels like a team. A moment with my college tennis team comes to mind. As a 20-year-old at our Duke matches, I often played a long three set singles match followed by a doubles match, sometimes another three sets. I remember losing some tough matches, but never because I was tired. But now, approaching my 71st birthday, my stamina is indeed an issue.

To complete the hour-long cardio clinic, one person plays on one side, trying to win a point, with the other three players rotating in, one after the other quickly. The person tries to stay out for two and a half minutes and win 10 points. Philip keeps the balls coming quickly, so basically it is three against one, a fresh opponent each point. By the end of my round, I cannot chase down the balls hit into a corner. I do finish the exercise without dropping out.

As I am leaving the clinic with the other Bill, I say, "You were hitting some nice balls out there."

"I've been hitting them for 63 years, since I was six years

old." He smiles. No more words, just a knowing space between us, an understanding of the magic of hitting a tennis ball over the net, even – or perhaps, especially, at 7 a.m., with a cold darkness outside.

Darkness and Light

That afternoon, at the local senior center, I lead a class called "Writing Your Spiritual Autobiography." To prompt ideas and reflections among the 10 participants, I read two poems by Danna Faulds. A section reminds me of the connections between a 70-year-old and a 10-year-old tennis player:

> But strength and weakness
> failure and success,
> faith and desolation –
> they are different ends
> of a single stick.

In 1957, in Jackson, Mississippi, I was a lost, lonely, and restless 10-year-old. I did not know what I felt at the time. But I did love hitting tennis balls. My tennis career has had its twists and turns through boyhood, college, tournaments in early adult years, and 35-and-over competitions. Then, my work life got busier, our kids were growing up, my wife stopped playing, and gradually, so did I. Now, after 30 years off from serious tennis, I'm back.

Writing with the others at the senior center that afternoon, I compose what is called an acrostic poem, using the first letter of a word as a structure, writing each letter on the page vertically. I choose the word "stick" from the Danna Faulds poem to serve as the start for the five lines of my acrostic poem. I call it "Divinity":

Solutions emerge like new growth
Together with rotting wood
I hold tight, feeling rough edges and smooth bark
Combining fears with hopes
Konnecting decades with darkness, openings with divinity.

If I had written an acrostic at age 10, I would never have felt the freedom to write "konnecting," so I could start the last line with a "k." While much changes over 60 years, some things stay the same. I still observe boundaries. I did use the letter "k" to honor the acrostic method but didn't mind spelling *connecting* with a "k." I smile at my departure, however slight, from the structures of life. Maybe I can learn a topspin backhand.

If I was lonely at age 10 – and that is how I picture that skinny boy – today I rarely feel that unchosen singularity. Solitude, yes. Loneliness rarely comes calling at this late-life juncture. I do face choices of communities. To play in the Thursday night tennis group, I choose to miss a regular meeting of a group of older men. Choices of communities, yes. But not isolation. So far, not loneliness.

Late in his life, at around age 90, my father lived alone in a small two-bedroom duplex at a retirement community. My mother had died about 18 months earlier. Occasionally, on our regular Sunday night telephone calls, he would say, "I do feel lonely sometimes." A strong man of spirit, he did not feel sorry for himself, but he did know about loneliness.

In reviewing how darkness visited me over the decades, I am grateful for tennis, which somehow helped keep the spark within me alive. Tennis games with grunting and gasping shape acquaintances into friendships, even for a brief time. Team members encourage each other, stroke after stroke. This comradery elevates my commitment, and my shot-making improves one ball after another.

At age 70, I need a new project to keep my body strong,

my community enriched, and my mind reflective. Tennis is the only life activity that I have done since age 10, along with a few other basics like reading. With tennis, I connect a body that still works well with a soul that resonates with the magic of hitting a little ball over a net. There is no logic to it, only a mingling of rough edges and smooth bark. With effort and friendship, in the end, darkness connects with divinity, with light.

• 4 •

A Serious Tennis Player

Saturday at 7 a.m., five days after the intense workout clinic, I am back on the indoor courts at another hour-long clinic. During a drill with four of us on the court, playing as doubles teams against each other, I hit a screaming forehand, barely clearing the center of the net. It dips and lands between the two guys on the other side, the perfect spot. Neither of them has time to make a stab at the ball. Instead, they both stand up and look at me. I feel the eyes of my partner, and the others in the back, ready to rotate into the drill, also land on me.

"Who are you?" asks the instructor, Philip, mocking the sound of an excited television announcer. "Were you some kind of pro?" Philip knows very well I am not a former pro; he saw me hit lots of mediocre shots during the workshop earlier in the week, which he also led. Then back to his normal voice, he adds, "Great shot, Bill."

Philip shares bits of advice as we go through singles and doubles drills that morning. "Give it more air over the net," he says to me. My forehands are mostly flat, with little topspin, which can lead to balls into the net. But when I hit it perfectly, the shot looks professional.

After the clinic, heading back home on this still early Saturday morning, I try to remember how I hit that shot. I did not know if I could still hit the ball that hard or with such precision. In fact, the ball went exactly where I aimed it with the speed I intended; it was not a fluke. Did the power come from a quick rotation of the hips and core, the torque? Did it come from racket speed, whipping through the ball? Did the pace come from stepping into it at just the exact moment with my full wiry, six-foot frame? I laugh, realizing I have no idea. I just swung from instinct. Then I laugh again, thinking: *Who would get out of bed on Saturday morning before dawn to chase balls on a tennis court, get winded, and test one's mettle against a bunch of other tennis players?* This morning, six guys did just that, in one tennis club in Raleigh, NC. Presumably, club-level players all around the country are doing something similar, having fun, trying to get better, being part of a tennis tribe.

Three days later, on December 19, I take the 7 a.m. intense workout clinic again. I hit good forehands, adding a little top-spin, but miss a lot of overheads. Bo is there again and encourages me when I again have to stop to catch my breath. But I do better than the week before. I am starting to become more of a tennis player, at least in terms of fitness.

Over the Christmas break, I think about how much I want to improve my technique. Do I want to learn to hit topspin forehands more consistently? And I have never had a reliable second serve. No one ever taught me how to hit an overhead. In fact, I have never really learned how to hit any of my shots from a professional. What are my goals in this new era of my tennis life? Do I want to start playing tournaments again, in the 70-and-over division? How good am I and how good can I become? I know I can get better.

As a kid I played on public courts, picking up bits and pieces about the game but mostly learning by playing. In college I had a little instruction from our volunteer assistant coach, a chemistry teacher. The paid coach administered the team but did not play; he was from the football staff and near retirement. In all my years of being around tennis, these clinics with Philip are my first with clear observation and suggestions from a professional instructor on how to improve my game.

After Christmas I see the advertisement for a six-session school at the Racquet Club, with each class focusing on a particular stroke. I decide to invest in my game.

In the first session, we focus on approach shots and volleys. When an opponent hits a short ball, not past the service line, a good strategy is to be aggressive, to take the ball early and hit it deep to your opponent's corner, an approach shot. Then try to win the point with a volley.

"Add topspin," Paul Henri, the young professional from France leading the sessions, tells me, as I hit my approach shots. "You need to get it over the net and deep. It does not have to be hard." Putting topspin on my approach does help me avoid hitting it into the net, but topspin is out of my comfort zone.

His tips on volleys reinforce what I have learned over the years playing doubles. But I have never thought exactly about basic tools that will improve my consistency. "Keep a tight wrist and the racket head above the wrist," he reminds us. "Pop it, punch it, don't swing."

Every session is packed with lessons and tips, all delivered as we hit ball after ball, refining the motions and footwork involved. He shows us where we might stand to receive serve, when to hop so we are ready to move into the service return, and when to run around the backhand in the ad court to hit more forehands. "Watch the pros on TV," he says as we catch our breath in one session. "See how they do it. It varies. Find out what works for you."

One session, Paul Henri draws a pyramid to illustrate a basic strategic approach to the game. The bottom level, used most frequently, is to keep the ball in play, hitting deep. The next level up is to be aggressive on short balls, usually coming to the net to set up the next shot. The third level up, playing with more risk and used less frequently, is to hit a sharp angle to put the player in trouble. And the top of the pyramid, used still less often, is to go for a winner.

He also has good advice on my strokes. "Your slice backhand can be more effective if you hit it deeper with more force." He does not try to teach me a topspin backhand, which I am happy about.

I make five of the six sessions and manage a make-up class during a two-week period. I also play a couple of singles and doubles matches. By the end of January, my head is crammed with possible adjustments to consider. And my body feels old. Six games in six days leaves me with a strain in my left quadricep and a recurring back ache.

Shortly after the six sessions end, I play a new opponent, David McCleod, who I have been told will be a good challenge for me. David runs me from corner to corner with his strokes and takes a quick lead. The short rest when we change sides of the court every two games is not enough. I cannot catch my breath. "I'm going to have to take a break. I'm embarrassed to be so tired."

David is patient with me, friendly. When we resume, he continues to win most of the points. My 6-1, 6-1 loss is discouraging. My leg hurts. My fitness needs way more work. And I need to get better all around. I'm not sure how to do any of this.

Maybe I should take some private lessons with Philip or Paul Henri. How much can I afford? And, how hard am I willing to work on improving my fitness and game? I have not sorted out my goal beyond just playing more tennis. I am making new friends with various doubles groups and some singles matches. One day, when I substitute in a new group, one player named Tio seems a bit older but still hits a good hard ball.

Later, I learn that Tio Campanile won the national 90-and-over Men's Championship the year before. I cannot believe Tio is 91 years old. Campanile picked up his first tennis racket in 1982, at the age of 55, when he switched from golf to tennis. Athletics came naturally to Campanile. He played hockey and basketball as a kid and baseball in college in his native Milwaukee. He played fast pitch softball into his late 40s. The tennis racket fit nicely into his hands. The serve seemed a bit like throwing a baseball. "It's a lifetime sport. I didn't start to play it until later because I was into team sports," he says.

The social aspects of the game and companionship of doubles groups at the Racquet Club became important as well as the competition. His wife of more than 60 years, Nancy, learned the game and played with groups of women at the club as well. The Racquet Club became a central focus in their lives.

A few weeks after the six-week class, Paul Henri gets a new job at another tennis club. With him gone, I wonder about talking with Philip about a private lesson or two. I run into him in the clubhouse. "You're starting to find a bit of your old form," Philip says. "Are you going to keep working on your game?"

"I'm not sure. Maybe I'll shoot for the National 90-and-over championship, like Tio." We both laugh. He knows I'm around age 70.

"Well, Tio is a great role model," Philip says.

Learning Topspin: A Commitment

By mentioning to a tennis pro that I aim to win the national 90-and-over championship, I realize I have put my first and only item on a bucket list. I have never believed in such a list, mainly, I suppose, because I have never felt like death was imminent. But now I am eight months into a new life, a life as a serious tennis player about to turn 71. But how serious am I really?

I no longer have the rigors of playing on a college tennis team as a focus. Nor am I seeking a boyhood adventure or an engaging diversion in my 30s. When the demands of work and family increased in my 40s, the diversion of tennis fell away. Now, in retirement and the last chapter of my life, where does tennis fit in?

The most famous and best-selling tennis book in history, *The Inner Game of Tennis*, is nearly 50 years old now. In it, Timothy Gallwey basically says to trust your inner self to hit the ball; his book is not about instruction on strokes but guidance for the inner voice. At the end, he writes: "Out of all the human experiences possible, which does the player of the inner game pursue? ... [O]nly when man is paying attention to something he really loves can he concentrate his mind and find true satisfaction."

At age 70 I joined a tennis club for the first time and followed the paths that became available. I sought out vigorous tennis clinics, met new friends, joined team tennis competitions, and found the groove of my old forehands and backhands. I can hit the ball hard and often true. I also know that I am woefully out of shape for tournament tennis, have not decided whether to refashion my strokes with topspin, and have not sorted out my goals for tennis.

Gradually I creep toward a decision line, the demarcation between hobby and commitment. One day, in a doubles game, I see one of my buddies taking a lesson from a pro named Carlos two courts down. Later I ask him how he liked the lesson. "Carlos is great," he says. "Nice to have an older guy. He coached a college team for a long time. He has lots of experience coaching, not just helping youngsters learn the game."

Through March and April, I keep playing singles and doubles, along with occasional clinics. I huff and puff in Phillip's early morning clinic and hit harder shots at another clinic, in drills with players rated 4.0 and 4.5. By April 9, exactly eight months after I joined the Racquet Club, I have played 79 times, about 10 times a month, twice as many doubles' games (42) as singles (21) with another 16 clinics or practice sessions (on a backboard, with the ball machine, or with another player hitting drills). What I have not done is hire a pro for individual lessons or enter any tournaments.

On May 24 I step onto the court with Carlos Garcia, tall and lanky, the oldest pro at the Racquet Club, in his late 40s. "I've seen you hit a little," he says as we head to the court. "I see you can hit the ball for sure. Let's warm up some and then talk a bit about what kinds of things you want to work on." I feel proud that I have made this commitment, to get help with my game, to spend retirement money on something I love.

During the hour lesson, he first gets a feel for the various parts of my game, and then we turn to footwork for my forehand. As a boy, I learned to hit a forehand by leading with my left front, which angles the torso to the right. Then the body can rotate toward the net, providing torque and power to the stroke. But in the last 20 years or so, that approach has evolved to what is called an open stance, where right-handers hit the forehand with both feet facing the net. The key is to turn the torso to get the same torque and power for the stroke without having to move the left foot around in front. "This saves steps and can make footwork more efficient," Carlos explains.

Next up – a topspin backhand. Trying an open stance on my forehand is a lot easier and more natural than a topspin backhand. Carlos walks me through the same basics that Malik went over in my free introductory lesson at the Club. I shift my grip on the racket slightly to the left so that the racket head initially tilts a little toward the ground.

I swing in an upward direction – not flat across my body – high toward the sky, following through above my right shoulder. The grip and motion create the topspin, with the ball going higher over the net and safely dropping into the backcourt. But if I do not commit fully to the high, upward swing with good speed, the ball lands into the net or even on my side of the court.

Lesson over, I think about how much work I'll need to integrate Carlos' points into my game. And I think about the tennis pyramid from Paul Henri. When to be aggressive, when to keep the ball in play. A lot to absorb. Meanwhile, I need to practice.

Six days later, I enter my first singles tournament.

● 5 ●

How Old is Your Friend?

Friday: My first match is scheduled for 5 p.m., June 1, 2018, Snow Hill, North Carolina. I leave my house in Raleigh at about 2:30 and head toward the rural counties to the east. I review three reminders for my opening match: keep the ball in play, commit to a specific shot, and remember "up and over" on my second serve (to avoid a double fault) and on low forehands (so I don't hit the ball into the net). I did not put my reminders on index cards, as John McEnroe did, stuffing them into the tennis bag he took on the court. Nor did I slide notes into my socks, as Jimmy Connors did, such as this one, "Don't forget to take the ball early."

Leaving the divided highway, I pass through tobacco, corn, soybean, and cabbage farms, and then through little Stantonsburg – population 784; 51 percent White, 45 percent African American. On this last leg into Snow Hill, I see the mesmerizing rows of young tobacco plants stretching to the horizon. African American men and women sit on a bench about six inches from the rich soil, backs bent to the earth in the 90-degree afternoon. Then I hit the outskirts of Snow Hill – population 1,595; 52 percent African American, 38 percent White – and see a tennis club on the right.

More pickup trucks fill the narrow parking lot than SUVs or high-end sedans, which are the usual models at the Raleigh Racquet Club. The cozy clubhouse has an informal, family-farm feel. A young woman checks me in. Later, I find out she's the daughter of Bobby Taylor, the tournament director, who designed and built the nine clay courts and clubhouse. A two-month-old baby, a lazy black lab, and others hang out in the large living room-like space.

The large maple behind court number 2 provides a shady spot for stretching: hamstrings, quads, inner thigh muscles, lower back, shoulders. I go through a simple routine, modifying yoga poses for the obvious muscles about to get their workout. I lather on HT 55 hydrogenic sun lotion, all over my face, neck, arms, and legs. Then, it's time to play.

Harry Spivey seems like he grew up from the soil, a friendly smile and handshake, easy gait as we walk together to the back set of courts, number 6 on the end. "I played on the high school team, near here," he offers as we put our tennis bags down in the shaded gazebo, with benches on each side for tired players to sit and sip water on changeovers. "I'm coming back after 15 years off from tennis," Spivey says. "Haven't really played since high school."

His fan base gathers in the corner just outside the fenced courts. A boy about 10 years old runs in and out of a small shade covering, like those portable little tent shelters people take to the beach. I glance at Spivey's friends and am surprised to see mostly African Americans, the youngster, a woman maybe in her 30s, and an older man, about my generation. Maybe an interracial relationship? A marriage? Eastern North Carolina unfolding in the 21st century.

Harry chats on, giving me more data for my mental preparation. I do the math, 18 years old at graduation plus 15 years off. I am facing a young man. But he appears heavier than a high school tennis player should. I wonder how he will move. The early summer heat wave leaves late afternoon temperatures in the 90s, higher if counting the humidity/heat index.

I hold back my data: turned 71 two weeks ago, came back to serious tennis 10 months ago when I joined the Raleigh

Racquet Club, played at Duke University (before scholarships), but haven't played in a singles tournament for 30 years, twice as long as my opponent. Harry hits nice topspin shots in the warmup. He learned tennis in the so-called modern era of new rackets, heavy topspins, and more attention to baseline rallies than serve and volleys.

For a few games, he does hit some good shots, and I miss enough to worry a little. I keep the ball in play and mostly commit to a shot (my internal index card). I aim for an area on the court with conviction and some power, rather than just pushing the ball back to the other side. I begin to take charge, building a 4-2 lead. I can sense him tiring, so I make sure to keep the ball in play. The first set ends two games later. He does manage an occasional beautiful topspin winner, but not enough to get more than a single game in the second set. So, a 6-2, 6-1 victory, the start to my new era of singles competition.

"I'm carrying around about 25 more pounds than I did in high school," Harry says as we walk to the clubhouse. "That didn't help me any. But you were the better player. Good luck."

Driving home, I recall my conversation with the tournament director the week before the entry deadline. "I'm an old guy who played a lot through college and in the 35-and-over division but have been off for 30 years," I said to Taylor, director of this 14th Annual Green County/Snow Hill American Red Cross Classic. "I'm a 3.5 in the system but play closer to 4.0 now. I'm thinking that since it's a men's division, I'll be better off at 3.5. What do you think?"

The U.S. Tennis Association uses a computer to rate players according to their ability. The rates go from 1.0 for beginners to 7.0 for world-class players. This tournament does not have a senior division.

"Well, a 3.5 guy in his 30s will definitely move better than a 3.5 guy in his 70s," Taylor said. "But the ages can vary a lot for the men's division. Let me look at who's registered so far."

I can hear him flipping through sheets of paper. "So far we have a teenager, guys in their 30s and 40s and 50s. The division you pick is up to you."

Saturday: In the quarterfinals, at noon, I play the teenager. The winner of our match is scheduled to play the semifinals at 6 p.m. Two matches, 90 plus degrees, 80-minute drive from home.

Bobby Taylor takes a low-key approach to sending people onto the courts. He spots me heading to the check-in table at match time and tells me which court. He points out a young man with dark hair, maybe 5 feet 6 inches, clearly not full grown yet.

James Rodriquez has the basics for what will be a very strong game one day, topspin strokes on both sides and a solid first serve. But his weak second serve proves too vulnerable; I attack it every chance I get. And I move to the net for easy winning volleys. Even so, he sometimes passes me down the line, or if I move too much in that direction, cross-court. The little guy has a game. But not enough. I catch onto his motion and begin to anticipate the direction. More volley winners. He is a baseliner. I attack at the net. He wins a lot of points. But I win more. In the end, I pump my fist when James floats his serve return wide on the first match point. I move on with a 6-3, 6-4 win.

"I played number 1 on the high school team," James tells me after the match is over.

"What grade are you in?"

"I just finished ninth grade." Good thing I didn't know that at the outset, I might not have taken him seriously, the ninth-grade part, not the number 1 part. I wasn't surprised to learn he played ahead of the other players that the Goldsboro High School team could field. Surely our age difference made some record for the tournament, maybe for any tournament ever held in North Carolina: 55 years separated us. But the old man persevered with enough guile, stamina, and commitment to his shots.

My shirt is soaked, my body is tired, and the heat penetrates the court and my body from noon until 1:15 or so when we finish. A hot game of tennis down east, summertime. What could be better! I need some food, shade, water, and rest before the semifinals.

The little patio outside the clubhouse becomes my resting place, with the two-person swing, random chairs and small tables, and a grill being readied for the evening hot dogs. I feel better from a shower but not yet whole. I pay attention to each crunch of the peanut butter sandwich I brought and the smooth, sweet taste of bananas from the box of tournament provisions. A big thermos of water, sip by sip, restoreth my pores. Shoes off, feet stretching, I watch a few random points from the four courts I can see. One other Raleigh Racquet Club member entered the tournament but left after his first-round loss on Friday. I am here alone, no friends, no family, no fans. My wife is away, pursuing her interests. I sit, eat, hear the thwops of balls hitting strings, and smell the sweat and hovering breath of summer heat. I soak in just being in tennis, breath to breath, my body trying to rejuvenate for another round with heat, humidity, and the honor of hitting a good serve and volley. Not to mention the lure of victory.

At 6 p.m., I head out again, to court 3 this time. Another friendly down east guy, John Turner, who slipped into the semis with a close win earlier in the day. When we start the warmup, I take a deep breath. Lefties can present some problems. So, fatigue, sun, and a leftie loom as my opponents.

Turner, I learn later, has been playing tennis only three years or so, but athletics shaped his tennis instincts. His quickness and nose for competition came from high school sports. And, somehow, in his short tennis career, he has learned a big kick serve, which seems to bounce high in unpredictable ways from his left-handed delivery. I try to block the ball back instead of catching it early and hitting through his spins (I needed that reminder from Jimmy Connors). The more cautious I am, the more his spins steer my balls far out of the court, easy points for him.

I am serving well and have enough energy to hit pressing groundstrokes, setting up some easy volley winners. But the sun still sears the court at 6:30 p.m. Attacking at the net takes a lot of energy. If a point lasts more than two or three shots, I can hardly catch my breath. My three opponents form a unified front: lefty serve, draining heat, and fading energy. He takes the first set 6-3. I am in serious trouble, barely hiding my exhaustion from Turner as I sit on the courtside gazebo before beginning the second set.

I drag myself off the bench, after deep and long gulps of water, to serve first in the second set. I promptly get behind as I watch balls go by me that normally I would chase down. As I struggle for energy, I notice the dark clouds peeling across the sky. No lightning yet but some distant rumbling of thunder.

A few sprinkles arrive. We play another point; I am behind 30-40. He is one point away from winning the first game, second set. Then the rain tumbles onto the courts like a huge waterfall. My opponent and other players grab their tennis bags and run for the clubhouse. I am too tired and sit hunkered down in the middle of the gazebo.

A woman from the match on the adjacent court is the only one of that doubles group who didn't sprint for the clubhouse. We are both catching our breath. "How are you doing?" she asks.

"Not so well. I lost the first set and am about to lose the first game of the second. I'm running out of steam. This sun is brutal. My second match today,"

"Well, the rain might give you the break you need," she says. We chat about tennis and sports and the fact that I'm from Raleigh. "I'm a big [NC State] Wolfpack fan," she says.

"My father played varsity basketball at State." She tells me of growing up in a sports-oriented family and her involvement in the area tennis scene as an adult. Finally, the rain lets up enough for us to walk over to the clubhouse. "Good luck with your match," she says. "I know you can come back! Bobby's courts dry quickly. You may be back on tonight."

I look at the puddles on the clay courts as I head back to the clubhouse and can't imagine playing again tonight. But then the sun comes out, hot as ever, and patches of clay began drying rapidly.

"We'll try to go back on in 45 minutes," Bobby Taylor says to various groups of players, some outside where the hotdog cookout has started. No way was I going to eat a hot dog at this point. I'm not sure I would keep it down if I had to start running after wide forehands again in 45 minutes.

One thing I know: I must get John Turner's high kicking serve back in play. But I'm not sure of the right strategy. I have time to kill, so I call Dick Heidgerd, my old doubles partner who shepherded me into the Raleigh Racquet Club. Besides being a tennis buddy, he knew something about lefties. In his 50s, when his right shoulder needed surgery after many years of hard serving, he got depressed. A friend, once a switch hitter in baseball, suggested he try playing left-handed. Dick was reluctant but gave it a try. Slowly, he improved so that he could even play on a club team. Just as happened when he got depressed in law school, tennis saved him, this time as a lefty. Dick says that playing left-handed – with some degree of excellence – was the best athletic achievement of his life and certainly the best of his tennis playing life.

"I need your advice," I tell him, explaining about the lefty serve kicking so high.

"Which way does it kick?" Dick asks. "Is it pulling you off the court on the deuce or ad sides?"

"You know, I can't really remember. I've gotten discombobulated by it and lost my focus on the return. I'm floating them back and mostly they float wide, guided by his spin."

Dick listens and then confirms my instinct. "I agree with you. You need to go after the return more aggressively, even if you miss some. At least you're controlling the point that way." And so, we agree, I will attack his big hops, taking the ball as it rises off the court before it gets up to six or eight feet high.

I stretch, trying to stay ready to play more as the sun keeps drying the courts. But then a second shower arrives, not as hard as the first but long enough to soak the courts again and make them unplayable that evening. Taylor again wanders among the lingering players. "All of those matches that were on the court will go back out at 8:30 tomorrow morning."

I change into dry shorts and t-shirt and head home past the tobacco fields. On the interstate, I see in the rear-view window what appears to be a thick, full rainbow. I pull over, put my hazard blinkers on, and gaze at the arch of bright colors across the entire sky, from one pot of gold to the other, every signature element as bright as, well, a real storybook rainbow. I smile, soaking in the beauty, then drag myself back into the Camry for the ride home. People in the parking lot at Whole Foods, where I stop to get dinner, are taking pictures of a rainbow – the same one or maybe another incarnation, an hour later and 65 miles to the west, horizon to horizon, thick, colorful, magnificent. I am a tired and happy old man.

Sunday: My stiff body feels every one of its 71 years at 8:30 a.m. I am serving at 30-40, first game of the second set, the score when the rains came yesterday. I focus hard to get my first serve in and pull out the game. Then I attack his high bouncing serve, mostly with success. My shots land in the corners, too strong for his still developing ground game. The second set is not close, 6-2. Like many USTA-sanctioned tournaments, the deciding set is called a super tiebreaker, the first person to get 10 points (leading by two) wins. Off we go, my confidence high, his spirit broken, a quick 10-3 victory.

"You were the better player," Turner says as we sit drinking water and toweling off. "You deserved to win."

"Maybe. But the rain saved me. Without the delay, I would not have pulled out that second set last night." He smiles, too polite to flat-out agree with me, but we both know the truth.

I take a shower, change clothes, and eat another peanut butter sandwich. Bananas are left in the clubhouse from last night, and I add ice to my thermos. I find a comfortable chair outside and wait.

On the court near the patio, an older man is playing a much younger guy, maybe a college student. It is the top-rated group (NTRP 4.5), and they have just split sets in a semifinal match. The older man comes to the patio to rest a few minutes before they begin the third set. He seems restless about something.

"I think I should retire," he says to me. "If I play on and win, I won't have anything left for the finals. I would hate to retire then before that match!" He pauses in this quandary and then announces his decision. "But I just can't retire." He takes a deep breath and heads for the court.

The sun is climbing high, heading for 90 degrees again at my second high-noon match in two days. Roger Swain, about 6-3, looks like a rangy high school quarterback. Besides being another lefty, the other surprise: he's African American, one of the few in the tournament. And he's from Charlotte, where big-time high school athletic programs have produced sports stars like Stephen Curry, one of the world's best pro basketball players. The tournament draws players primarily from the eastern counties, except the finalists in the 3.5 men's division, Raleigh old man versus Charlotte ex-athlete.

In the warmup, he hits his serve hard and flat, as if rifling a pass to the endzone. His strokes lack the smooth history of a childhood tennis career, but he's proven his number one seed in the 3.5 draw, losing just a few games in both the quarterfinals and the semis.

He wins the toss and chooses to receive. He must've read the same tip in *Tennis* magazine: better to get nerves out of the way on the first game without losing your serve. I lose my serve. His first service game, he booms in four straight first serves. But I am used to hard hitters from playing doubles indoors over the winter. The pace doesn't bother me like the spin. I block his first serves back. Then he hits a weak second serve, like those of the teenager two rounds back. I jump on Swain's second serve with a knowing smile, following my deep return to the net and put away a volley when he floats a return up the middle. We keep this pattern up, each breaking the other's serves until it's 4-4.

Then I hit what looks like a clean ace to me, at deuce, down the middle, right on the middle line. I assume I've won the point and start to walk over to the ad court to serve for the game.

"Out," he calls without hesitation.

I stop and look up, surprised. "Are you sure?"

Now *he* is taken aback. "It's my call," he snaps back. "I call the balls on my side." He delivers that piece of common knowledge like a smashing volley when a simple dink would have done.

What is this extra zing? Maybe the tension of the final, a close first set, the heat, the fact that his power serve isn't bothering me. But what zips across my radar screen is race, especially white privilege. Here's the only African American man in our division – perhaps in this entire rural, down-east, pickup truck tournament – and I'm questioning his call. Is he insulted? Angry about my privilege, having grown up with tennis? He's an athlete. He can see from my smooth strokes that I learned this game as a kid.

I think about saying, "Would you mind looking at the mark at least?" But I hold my tongue. If race played any part in his mind, consciously or not, no follow-up question is worth it. I go back to the deuce court for my second serve.

McEnroe or Connors would not have let it go. But they played for much higher stakes, of course, even as kids, and they did not care about their manners – they say that in their memoirs. Arthur Ashe would never have asked for another look at a line mark. His mentor in Virginia, who catapulted him into big-time tennis in the 1960s, taught him never to question a call and to be polite.

Without that ace, I lose my serve for the fifth straight time. He serves for the first set at 5-4. But he can't pull out his first service game win either. Back to 5-5, and I lose my serve, sixth time in a row. Frustration joins with the heat to wilt my energy and will. The serve takes a lot of effort, physical and mental: toss, extend the right arm, bend the knees, uncoil and snap the wrist at the right time, all directed toward a spot in the service box. Coming back to tennis after so many years, even after playing doubles regularly for about nine months now, I need to focus on the body mechanics. Serving now at 6-5, Swain keeps the ball in play longer than I do, running me from side to side. I run out of steam and points. First set to Swain, 7-5.

At first, no one seems to be watching our match. But as the first set moves along, I notice two guys following our points from the shelter between the two sets of courts. Then, John Turner, my semifinals opponent, joins them. When I move over to that side of the court, I make eye contact with them, and they seem to be in my camp. No fist pumps or cheers, just quiet support, I think. Or maybe they just wanted to see a close final.

Finally, the first set over, I virtually collapse onto the gazebo bench. I am thinking about retiring but know I can't do that. "I just came to get some water," I tell Swain as he arrives at the gazebo. "I know I'm back on the same side to start serving." These are the first words we exchanged since I questioned his call on my serve. We sit quietly now, drinking water. I put on a dry t-shirt and pull myself back to the side near what I now consider my fan base.

I can hardly muster the energy for a true serve, so I try to spin in a second serve. I do get the serve in, but Swain's return heads for the backhand corner. Normally, I would take two quick steps, plant my right foot, and at least slice a return, if not hit a harder flat stroke crosscourt. All I can do is stand and watch. His next return passes me by as if I am a spectator. Only when his shots are within a single step can I hit them back. First game to Swain. I head for the gazebo, more water and rest. The two games on the far side, away from my fans, are the same, even quicker. Back to the gazebo, down 0-3. Now I am thinking, is a 6-0 loss or retiring more embarrassing for my first tournament back?

I remember the visit of the older man at the patio, his dilemma about whether to retire. Suddenly, I feel like a representative of older men – *I can't retire*! Slowly, I trudge toward the baseline to receive serve. Swain is still hitting his hard serve, and I return a couple, my best shot now. I lack the strength to attack his second serve or reach his shots in the corners. An idea comes to me: try hitting some drop shots. I win one point with a drop shot, but he still moves to 4-0, second set. Again, I'm to serve.

My first serve falls weakly into the net and rolls back a few feet. Normally, I would go and get the ball to have a clear court before I serve the second ball. *What's the difference? It's 0-4 and I can hardly walk.* I assume my stance and bounce the ball, about to hit my second serve. But then, something deep inside stops me. I look at the ball near the net and move towards it. I walk slowly and stop, hit it to the back fence with the edge of my racket – lacking energy even to lean down or bounce the ball up to my hand. Back to the service line now, I glance at my fan base, and they are with me, I know it. I win the point. Another point. Another drop shot. Swain runs it down, but I am ready for his weak shot, and I lob it over him. He runs that down too. I drop-shot him again. I win the game. Side change, Swain serving at 4-1.

My drop shot and lob are my weapons. And I manage to attack his weak second serve. I win both games on the side of the court away from my fans. We change sides again. Now, I have the momentum, winning three straight games. This set is no longer his for the taking. But he's caught on by now, anticipating the drop shots. I try to mix in some strokes but lack the energy to muscle them with any power. He moves to 5-3 with his service game.

I gather up the balls to serve, my fans behind me. "It's not over 'til the fat lady sings," I say to them, my first communication with the three guys who are on the edge of their seats now. They smile but still no fist pumps or comments. Just polite, down-east good old boys, enjoying a hot Sunday afternoon of tennis.

The game seems easier now. My serves arrive at Swain with a little hop. I stroke the ball with some pace. I hit one surprise drop shot, another lob. Swain is hustling his big body up and back. But not enough. I hold serve. We change sides. He's serving for the match now, at 5-4. My comeback in spirit carries me further than I think I can go, but he has energy and strokes left. Finally, on the final point, he hits a drop shot himself – a strategy he began the last few games as well. It's a good one and requires all I have left just to reach it. Few 71-year-olds in the state of North Carolina, near the end of their second match of the day would've even reached his dropper. I barely get my racket on it, which leads to a pop up. He lines up his forehand, a sweeping left-handed stroke, and crushes it down the line, well out of my reach.

"Yes!" He jumps up with relief and joy. He has not let the match slip away, even when his 4-0 lead went down to 5-4 in the second set. We shake hands and chat for the first time since we walked out 90 minutes earlier.

"The first set was something else," he says. "I said to myself, the first person to hold serve will win the set, and that's exactly what happened."

He heads for the clubhouse to get his winner's trophy before driving back to Charlotte. I shuffle out the back gate to the little shelter where my fans are still sitting. They congratulate me on my comeback. "Maybe I'll see you at another tournament," I say to John Turner as the group goes back to the clubhouse.

I sit there, resting, watching the finals of the 4.5 division, the older man holding his own with a smooth-hitting college player. Soaking wet and sipping water, I can't force myself to get up. The woman who hunkered next to me in the gazebo during the rain delay comes out to keep me company. "You were out there a long time," she said. "Are you OK?"

"Yeah, I'm just winding down, catching my breath. The match took a lot out of me."

I ask her about the older man who won his semifinals match and is now playing in the finals on the court near us. "Oh, he's 57 now," she tells me. "And he's playing a college kid."

About that time, he comes over near us walking down a ball that came over from his court. He sees his friend in the bleachers chatting with me. He has seen me struggle at the end of my match, as he is hanging on himself in this hot weather. "How old is your friend?" He gestures with his head toward me.

"He's 71," she says.

He picks up the ball and smiles before he heads back to serve in his finals. "That's what I want to be at that age."

6

Courting Colleagues

Monday morning, 9 a.m., after three days of commuting to the Snow Hill tournament and enduring some exhausting moments on the court, I am back for more. I have my second lesson scheduled with Carlos at the Racquet Club. Poor planning for my body, which could use some rest, but even so, I am glad to get back on this track of professional guidance. We work on forehand preparation, attacking short balls and the follow-up footwork for a volley. He tinkers with my grip so I can hit a slice volley, and we spend some time on my bugaboo, a topspin backhand. The next day, I hit against the ball machine. Then on Wednesday, hit crosscourt and down-the-line drills with a playing partner. Finally, Thursday, I take off!

On Friday, I play in a light doubles group, not too strenuous and not too high a level. Good practice for keeping the ball in play and facing different types of opponents. And, I get to play with Tio, my role model for that mythical goal of a 90-and-over national championship! All is going well. About mid-way in the match, I casually prepare to receive Tio's serve – he is 91 after all. I am playing the ad side of the court on the left. Often, a server aims for the outside part of the service box in the ad court, forcing a right hander (most players) to hit a backhand.

Tio makes his toss and I lean to my left, preparing for a

backhand. But he guides a hard flat serve straight down the middle of the court, just inside the service box. I stop my leftward lean and shift the other way, barely stabbing at the ball, but do manage a weak forehand return. Tio comes in off his serve and attacks my short return with a wicked drop shot back my way. I take off from behind the baseline and run it down just before the ball makes a second bounce, slapping the ball across for a winner.

"You have legs," Tio says, shaking his head as he loses the point. "But how long can they work!" We laugh. He knows I hope to make the 90-and-over division in another 20 years or so.

"Well, I don't know about my legs. But I sure am glad a 90-year-old didn't ace me today. It was close." We laugh some more. Playing with Tio, I realize he has far more than just amazing physical abilities for his age. His humor, joy in being around the other players, and goodwill during the game is contagious. He loves being on the court and with his friends.

"I have been disciplined, using regular exercises to keep muscles and joints working well," he tells me. He cites research (now well known in tennis circles) that found tennis players live longer than most people, even other athletes like joggers, due to the combination of exercise and social contact. "Recognizing the value of tennis has encouraged me to maintain a level of activity that otherwise I wouldn't get," he says.

For most people, awards come earlier in life, maybe in your prime as an athlete or in retirement in business, Tio says. "I've had the reversal. Getting rewarded in the twilight of my life is very satisfying, with the greatest trophies, national championships. Tennis is a competitive, athletic activity that has served me very well – it was a way to meet so many people as a part of my life."

Role Models and Motivation

Tio is not the only role model that offers me good lessons and motivation. Throughout the summer, I keep working on my game, preparing for two bigger tournaments that are coming up, the NC State Championships the last weekend in August, and the National Clay Court Championships in October. I play with singles partners, take lessons from Carlos, and attend clinics. I make new friends at the Raleigh club and a tennis club in nearby Durham.

One of the players at the Durham club, Jimmy Washington, has been playing in the national clay court tournament for several years. With shoulder-length white hair and a beard, Jimmy is six years my senior. Younger legs should give me an advantage, but Jimmy has experience and a quirky tenacity. He hits a hard slice forehand, a shot few others hit, as well as the more familiar slice backhand. To get his slices back over the net, I have to bend lower than usual since the ball is skimming across the court rather than bouncing up to my racket.

"I learned the slice growing up on a farm in northeastern Alabama," he tells me one day. "My father and other farmers gathered around a field that they would use as a tennis court." They often played in their work clothes and with warped rackets, since most of them did not have presses to keep the old wooden rackets from bending, Jimmy explains. "I watched these guys use the warp in their old rackets to hit odd spins, using the concave curve for one kind of spin and the convex curve for another. And that's where I first played tennis."

In one of our matches, we split the first two sets. To win the third, I dip low for his slices and fight through fatigue, finding an unexpected level of fitness. Meanwhile, Jimmy hardly seems winded. This is his 13th consecutive day for a tennis match. Last month, he played 28 days. Most seniors I know play at most three days a week, sometimes four.

"Why do you keep this torrid pace?" I ask as we wind

down after our match.

"Simple," he says, "to feel better. Health is huge. There is natural depression in my family, even when I was a kid. When I do something physical, I have always been able to feel good as a consequence." A second reason follows quickly but takes a little longer to explain.

"I have had a lifelong quest for knowledge of how the universe works," he begins. "Tennis is part of that. If I can improve how I play tennis, then tennis helps me answer questions about knowledge." For about 20 years now, Jimmy has kept logbooks of each of his matches, writing about stroke adjustments, string tension, grip size, racket weight, top-spins, slices, defensive strategies, when to attack, nutrition, stretch regimens. "I consider tennis to be part of my research and thinking, my philosophy," he says. "Tennis is a lab, a scientific process."

His cumulative notes now fill a stack of notebooks two feet high. "Winning or losing is not my purpose," he says. "But it is a motivator for determining whether I am improving or not." Then he points to outcomes from his journey, just as a scientist talks about evidence-based interventions.

When he started playing tournaments, he was 17th in the state in the 60-and-over division. He kept practicing and making changes, drawing on his tennis instincts and self-taught adjustments, always learning more new tricks, as he calls his different ways of playing. "I wanted to know if my methods were working." He climbed to the top of the North Carolina ranking in the 60s and over. He moved up to the next age division and never looked back, finishing third and then second in national championships – so far.

In the clinics at the Racquet Club, I meet another good player, Mike Stewart, at a 7 a.m. clinic for 4.5-level players. I am delighted to see another man there with whitish-gray hair, lean and hard hitting, a lot like me. As we go through the drills and then play doubles in the clinic, I also see Stewart's concentration and competitive streak. He likes to attack the ball and to win, even in practice points in a clinic. We decide to play some singles.

Walking to the court for our first match, Mike says, "I'm a better doubles player than singles." I look over and sense a combination of playful banter, as athletes are apt to do, as well as perhaps a bit of truth. I pull my racket from my tennis bag and say, "Well, I'm glad I should have the advantage today, since we're playing singles." We both laugh. Then we play a close match, each of us winning a set.

As a boy, little Mike Stewart won most ping pong games at the local YMCA in Louisville, Kentucky. Then, at around age 12 or 13, he found a set of public tennis courts in a city park not far from his house. "I was pretty good with any kind of racket and ball," he says, as we wind down from our match.

Some 50 years after he picked up a tennis racket, he was the best not just in Louisville or at the Raleigh Racquet Club but in his age group in all the land. He won his first national championship in the 65-and-over division in doubles, winning what the U.S. Tennis Association calls a "gold ball." In the last 15 years, Mike has won about 20 gold balls in the 65-, 70-, and 75-and-over age divisions, as well as the father-son division, and scores of silver balls (second place). On the international level, he has won two World Championships in doubles.

"When I won my first gold ball, I changed," he says. "I realized that these guys [at the top] are not untouchable. Once you know that you're in that class, you get over a hurdle. Then, you expect to win."

Getting better in tennis is like much of life, he says. "In my first job, I wasn't great but got better at it. Same with tennis. I gradually got better. Being self-taught, the disadvantage was that I had to learn everything," he says. "But the advantage was that you have to know the nuances of all the shots."

Competition and winning are not the only parts of tennis that motivate Mike. "The social side of tennis is important. A lot of friendships develop from the tournaments and playing at the clubs. And, of course, tennis is great for staying healthy."

What else has he learned from tennis? Stewart ponders that question for a moment. "Integrity. On the court, making the calls. You have to give your opponent the benefit of the doubt. If the shot isn't clearly out, you have to call it in. Integrity is an important part of the game."

Motivation for the upcoming tournaments – and maybe a long-term run in this thing called senior tennis – can come in unexpected ways. One day in a practice match, I notice an older woman hitting volleys on the court next to me. Gisela Grace stands two feet from the net, holding a classic ready position, racket head above her wrist, knees slightly bent. She is prepared for the balls a young tennis pro is hitting at her.

Gisela is enjoying her first love, tennis, even as her Alzheimer's disease advances. Scientists believe that music activates the memory of those with this disease. For Gisela, tennis was her music. She started hitting tennis balls at age six in her native Brazil. Her body memory is evident that day on the court next to me – stiff wrist to control a volley, slice motion to keep the ball in the court. She volleys as well as someone 50 years younger. When her hitting session ends, Gisela's husband of 54 years, John, comes up and guides her arm into her jacket.

One day, I join John and Gisela for lunch in the Racquet Club grill, along with their daughter visiting from Tennessee. Gisela does not talk but she smiles, especially when I mention Maria Bueno, who won Wimbledon several times and reached number one in the world. In the 1950s, Gisela played with and against Bueno many times when they were both youth champions in Brazil.

Even as her Alzheimer's disease progressed, "Gisela remained mostly happy and optimistic and a joy to be with," John says. Her tennis posture when she hits her volleys reflects that joy. Tennis is truly a sport for life.

North Carolina State Championships

Over the summer, I work at my game: lessons with Carlos, a weekly clinic, matches with Jimmy in Durham and Mike and others at the Raleigh club, and another doubles match with Tio's group. I'm feeling confident as I prepare for my first-round match in the NC State Championships, 70-and-over division.

On Friday, August 31, 2018, when I take the court at 5 p.m., the sun is still bright with 90 degrees heat along with 50 percent humidity. A friend from the Racquet Club, Keith Sipe, is beside me. We were not happy to draw each other for a first round match; it's always hard to play a friend. From our practice matches over the summer, we both know I should win this match. But just a few weeks ago, both sets were close. If I tighten up, I could lose.

From the first point, I focus hard. Keith likes to talk to opponents during changeovers because he's a friendly guy, not as a strategy to break their concentration. I stay silent when we sit for a few minutes, changing courts and drinking water; I am determined to win this first match in a big tournament and do not want to be distracted. He senses my approach and keeps the chit-chat to a minimum. Finally, after losing the first set and down 0-3 in the second, he starts talking.

"Look, Bill, we both know I'm not going to come back now," he says as we gulp water, the sun still bitterly hot, now close to 6 o'clock. You're playing great, way too strong for me. I nod. I'm going for my shots and hitting the corners. I roll through the next three games for a convincing first round win.

The next morning, 9 a.m., the sun is beating down already at 90 degrees, as if it never went to sleep. It is back to torture me as I take the court against the second-seeded player, Richard Shipman. Seeded above my friend Jimmy Washington, Shipman may be a notch above my level.

"How good is Shipman?" I ask Jimmy as we mingle, waiting for the Saturday morning matches to start.

"Well, I've never beaten him," Jimmy says. "And I've played him a lot of times."

During the warmup, Shipman hits smooth deep strokes and solid serves but nothing overwhelmingly hard. I sense he is steady and challenging but not unbeatable. I win the toss and choose to serve first. I don't want to get behind from the start. I'm serving well and think I should be able to get the first game.

I win the first several points, but he hits sharp, deep returns and takes the first game to deuce. Then we begin a long, back-and-forth of ads and deuces. He gets the ad – called a "break" point (to break my service game) – but I hold him off. Then I get the ad but can't close out the game. Finally, in what must have been a 15-minute game, he hits a winner beyond my reach. Even before it's 9:30 in the morning, I'm soaking wet from one game. I sit and try to stay calm, not happy about losing that game.

"That seemed more like a set than a game," Shipman says, breathing hard himself. I nod and mutter something like, "Yeah, sure did." I can tell he's not trying to break my concentration, just being friendly.

The next several games are close and hard-fought. But I can't get that service break back. We play out the first set with no more service breaks after that first game. Even though I had overnight to recover from my previous match, my body cannot bounce back for a second tough set against an opponent like Shipman. He sends me from corner to corner on many points. My legs tire, and my breath is shallow. I start to fade.

Shipman moves through the second set easily. We shake hands and chat going back to the clubhouse. I feel like I played well and can compete with the best players in the state. But I need more stamina, more consistency, and, most importantly, more belief in myself.

● 7 ●

National Clay Court Championships

On a beautiful October Sunday, several weeks after the State Championships, I make the 90-minute drive from Raleigh to Pinehurst, NC. I am excited to be entering my first national tournament, and nervous: the USTA Men's National Clay Court Championships, 70-and-older division. My game has steadily improved over the summer, and while disappointed with my loss at the state tournament, I felt good about my performance. I feel confident in my first-round match against another unseeded player.

The tennis courts lie on both sides of the picturesque drive into the Pinehurst Country Club, famous in golf circles for hosting the U.S. Open. I spot a shady area near the parking lot for stretching and warming up muscles. Then, I join others hitting strokes on practice courts.

Body loose, strokes ready, I mingle with the crowd of guys with gray and white hair, standing around a large tent. Tournament officials are checking the drawsheets behind makeshift desks under the tent. New cans of balls, open and ready for action, cover a second desk.

Announcements are coming now for the early afternoon matches. Hearing their names, old men grab tennis bags and water bottles before picking up their can of balls. "Mr. Finger," the official calls out. I move past the box of bananas and stacks of white towels on the desk next to the drawsheets. My opponent and I introduce ourselves and head to the near set of courts where I had just hit my warm-up balls. Footsteps and sliding marks from the warmup have been brushed away, lines clear white once again. The pristine court is ready for action.

In the allotted five-minute warmup, any remaining feelings of novelty for a national tournament fall away into familiar forehands and backhands. My opponent, who comes from the Atlanta area, hits an easy, steady ball. If I limit my unforced errors, I can produce more power than he can handle.

Early in the first set, I take charge and win enough points for a comfortable lead. But as the set moves toward the end, my nerves lead to errors, and the score remains close. *Don't blow this chance to move into the next round*, I am thinking. I focus more on keeping the ball in play while still making enough aggressive shots that he cannot return. I get through the first set, winning 7-5. In the second set, I am more relaxed and hit with more pace and consistency, easing through for a 6-2 win. Walking to turn in the score and balls, I am smiling and thinking, *I can, in fact, compete in a national tournament.*

As I report the 7-5, 6-2 win, I see guys lingering around the tent but don't know any of them. I head home and will get to bed plenty early for the next round in the morning.

On Monday, arriving in the Pinehurst parking lot, I see Jimmy Washington, my friend with the slice shots and tall stack of tennis notebooks. We chat about our opponents as we put on tennis shoes and sort out extra shirts in our tennis bags.

"I play Norm Chryst, one of the guys seeded number five," I say. The tournament seeds the four best players number one through four, and then four more guys get a number five seed without ranking them. Finally, eight more guys get a number nine seed. In total, there are 16 seeded players in a tournament draw of about 64 players. I ask Jimmy, "Do you know Chryst?"

"Have known him for years," Jimmy says. "Chryst has been around big-time tennis for a long time. He used to be an umpire on the professional circuit. Has called some big matches, even in grand slams. He has a high tennis IQ and is a crafty player. But he is not going to overwhelm you."

I soak in this information, stretching and warming up my legs, knowing I need to play with confidence, using my best shot – a forehand to the backhand corner – whenever I can. The buzz of old men chatting around the tent seems a little more relaxed today. Before I get into any conversation, I hear Chryst's name called and head to the officials' table.

Chryst is friendly enough walking to the match, on a new set of courts for me. When we reach our court, though, the chit chat ends. Towels and rackets out, water bottles ready. The day is already warm. He wins the toss and chooses to receive serve for the first game. Pressure immediately falls on me to hold serve, which should, in theory, be an advantage.

I hit some deep serves with some hop, forcing him into challenging backhand returns. We have several good cross-court forehand rallies. I realize I'm nose-to-nose in this first game with one of the best players in the tournament. We come to our third deuce. My unforced error gives him another advantage point. Then I miss a first serve. He steps into my softer second serve and hits a winner, claiming the first game.

As we cross sides of the court, sipping water, I could feel his glance over at me. *Who is this guy?* he seems to be thinking. Since it's my first national tournament, he's never heard of me. He realizes that I am not a walkover. I scoop up my racket, breathe the morning air, and head for the opposite side of our court. I will try to attack his serves, following a few returns into the net for volleys. My aggressive play works, and I break his serve to level the score at 1-1.

Again, I need to hold serve to maintain the advantage of serving first. But his sharp, angled cross-court shots force errors from me, and he breaks my serve again. Now serving at

2-1, Chryst again faces some sharp returns from me and cannot consolidate his second straight service break. No service holds yet, and I pick up confidence, tying the first set at 2-2.

The next game, I hit two blistering cross-court backhand winners as he approaches the net. All he can do is watch the ball whistle by. I take a 3-2 lead, finally holding serve. Then he also holds serve for the first time, tying the score at 3-3.

Jimmy told me in the parking lot that Chryst has game plans for matches, sometimes shifting to a new strategy if the first plan is not working. As I step back to serve at 3-3, Chryst must have gone to a Plan B. He interrupts my attacking game by attacking me first. He shifts, I slowly realize, to what some would call a brand of "old-man" tennis. After returning my serve, he moves toward the net but pauses halfway between the service line and baseline, usually considered a so-called "no-man's land." While kids learn to stay out of this area, a skilled senior player like Chryst can pick off strokes with volleys from there and direct them to the corners. They are not traditional winning volleys but do put me in a difficult defensive position. His strategy works, breaking my serve and then holding for a 5-3 lead. Again, I cannot handle his attacks on my serve and his strategy hitting from no-man's land. I lose a close first set 6-3.

I head to my bench as we change sides, taking deep draws from my water bottle and finding a dry shirt in my bag. It's October, but feels like August, with the temperature approaching 90 now. I breathe in the damp, humid air.

The second set begins as tight as the first. Serving to try to level the set at 2-2, the score moves to deuce. I bounce the ball calmly, aim for his backhand, but chase a short toss and hit it into the net. Second serve. Deep breath. I tell myself, *up and over*. I make a high toss, but I do not snap my wrist to pull the ball down into the service box. I send the second serve well long. Double fault, advantage to Chryst. Next point, a bad carbon copy. Tried too hard on the first serve, not up and over, and it lands in the center of the net. Careful but tight on the second serve, it lands just long. Two double faults in a row, he takes the lead at 3-1.

We continue to have a lot of deuces and ads, but he keeps winning the key points, again and again. I hit one of my signature and most reliable shots, a slice backhand down the line. But rather than skimming over the net, as this shot does at home, I hit the top of the net and wince as the ball falls back on my side. I need more air over this highest part of the net. Aggressive yes. But not safe enough, not enough "air" between the net and my ball. Tennis is a game of inches.

As he continues to win the key points, he has momentum. Now, deep into the second set, he seems to add what might be Plan C, drop shots and lobs. Early in the match, I chased down several of his drop shots, returning some for winners with nifty forehand drops of my own angled sharply, almost parallel to the net. But now, he anticipates my forehand cross-court and is waiting. This time, he pops the ball over my head for a winning lob. The drop shots keep coming, mixed with lobs. I try to anticipate them and vary my return, scrambling, hanging on. But Chryst plants himself in no-man's land after his drop shots, covers my best returns, and at several key moments, lofts lobs over my head. I turn and simply stare, helpless, after racing to the net for his drop shot. Chryst goes to a 4-1 lead.

I try to settle myself to hold serve, trying to forget how I ended my last service game – two straight double faults. But the memory creeps into my body motion anyway, stronger than my confidence in a second serve. I repeat what no tennis player wants to do: two more double faults, now four in a row, over two service games. But I breathe deep, steady myself, and hit good shots, and get the game back to deuce. Giving away free points to a player as smart as Chryst is too much of a disadvantage. He smells the final handshake now and wraps up the match at 6-1.

"That felt a lot closer than the score," he says as we towel off and gulp water. "Something like four and four."

I linger beside the court as Chryst walks to the officials' tent to report the score. I feel proud that I played a hard match, thinking over those critical double faults that cost me dearly. Those two games when I lost serve turned the match his way. *Looking competitive in points is not good enough*, I'm thinking. Still, I did fine for my first national tournament. And, I have the consolation bracket ahead.

Settling into the Tournament Crowd

After a shower, I linger on the patio between the clubhouse and the stadium court, listening to players swap tales of matches, injuries, and families. Many of them participate in these national tournaments regularly. I'm in no hurry to leave now and want to learn more about the circuit of old men's tennis tournaments.

My friend Keith, who I played in the state tournament, is telling me what a good match I played and lamenting his own loss. Like our mutual friend, Jimmy, he has played many tournaments in the senior divisions in recent years and knows many of the players. He introduces me to Art Abbott, a regular at these tournaments.

Art and I say hello. "I understand you played at Clemson about the same time I played at Duke. I'm trying to remember if we played each other." Both schools were in the Atlantic Coast Conference and played each other every year.

"I don't think so," says Abbott. "I don't remember the Duke matches. We didn't worry much about Duke. We worried about Carolina." Clemson and the University of North Carolina were by far the two best teams in the conference.

"You guys had a bunch of players from other countries, didn't you?" I ask. "I remember a tall, lanky American guy too.

I played him once in the summer."

"Was that in Augusta, Georgia?" Abbott asks.

A picture of that match in Augusta, Georgia, snaps into my memory, another hot day on clay courts 50 years earlier. "That's right, now that you mention it. I didn't even wear socks in the match for some reason. Probably because I played that way all summer, running the tennis program at a boys' camp." I catch my breath, thinking that this stranger beside me somehow remembers a match I played after my sophomore year in college in 1967.

"How could you possibly remember that match?" I ask Abbott.

"Nobody beat David Cooper like you were doing at first. So I remember it."

"I do remember jumping ahead," I say. "I was on fire, loose, hitting winners. I was ahead about 5-2 in the first set, something like that." The picture of this scruffy camp counselor going toe to toe against an accomplished champion tennis player comes into clear focus.

"I'm pretty sure you didn't win that first set," Abbott says. "He didn't lose many."

I talk with several other regulars at the tournaments and study the large bracket on the wall of the clubhouse, learning the names of the top seeds and how they are doing. Chryst will move on to play in the round of 16 now, playing another seeded player. Then I study the consolation bracket, where I will now compete. This tournament feeds losing players into another bracket, which allows for lots more matches between people from all over the country. I look at my draw for tomorrow and hope for the best.

On Tuesday morning, I play a relatively weak player from the Baltimore area. He gives me too many soft second serves, and I hit winner after winner. On my serve, no double faults and few unforced errors. The match isn't even as close as the lopsided final score: 6-0, 6-1. I am scheduled for another round in the consolation bracket at noon, again under unseasonal summer-like heat, and my third singles match in just over 24 hours.

This time, I go against David Reid, an unseeded player at about my skill level. My friend Keith knows him from previous tournaments. "He's from Florida, a very nice guy," Keith says as I wait for the match to begin. "He's a solid player, but you can beat him."

The August-like heat arrives at the noon starting time, along with us two old guys, fighting for our survival in the consolation bracket. Perhaps playing my second match of the day affects my early concentration. Whatever the cause, I lack focus in the first set and cannot get my power strokes into rhythm. Reid senses that all he needs to do is keep the ball in play, and he does, taking the first set 6-2.

In the second set, I make better decisions, giving Reid fewer free points. I wait for an opening before going for a winner. The set moves back and forth. I'm in the match now, but am tiring in the heat. Reid serves for the match at 5-4. The game goes to deuce several times.

The afternoon heat seems to be spiking another 10 degrees as sweat pours off me. *Hang in there*, I tell myself. *Break his serve now and get to the tiebreak.* If I can get the score to 5-5, maybe I can pull out the second set. In the consolation matches, a 10-point tiebreaker is used instead of a full third set. I could somehow summon enough energy for that. But he buckles down, not wanting to go further and pulls out the game and the match, 6-2, 6-4.

"You should play more of these tournaments," he says as we shake hands.

My tournament is over.

Sagging Body and Spirit

After the match, I eat lunch in the little one-block downtown area of Pinehurst with Jimmy and Keith, my two buddies from

Durham. They have also lost in the 70s division, main draw and consolation bracket. We swap stories of our matches over crab cake sandwiches and cold drafts. Then they head home, and I amble through a small street of historic homes back to the Pinehurst Country Club and its beautiful tall pines. I watch more tennis to pass some time before the tournament banquet, which is scheduled for Tuesday night. My body aches and my spirit is sagging.

I feel a bit forlorn and alone, saturated with tennis, not sure if I did well or should have done better. I won two and lost two, beating players I should have beaten and losing to good players. But I could have won more, I think.

I move my car up the drive from the tennis area to a shady section of the parking lot near the dinner location. I push the lever on the driver's seat, lean back and close my eyes. Maybe winning isn't everything. An hour or so later, I wake up and stretch.

People are already finding places to sit with their friends when I step into the banquet room at the Pinehurst Country Club. I see my friend from the Raleigh Racquet Club, Tio Campanile. He is sitting with his usual smile, and his wife, Nancy, of more than 60 years, is beside him.

"Anyone sitting here?" I ask, my hands on the chair beside Nancy.

"You are," Tio says, welcoming me as if we were back at the Racquet Club in the Friday morning doubles group where I play with him occasionally. "I'm glad you're here, Bill," Tio says, his broad face as welcoming as a kind uncle. I join Tio and Nancy.

Earlier in the day, Tio won the national singles championship in the 90-and-over division, with a dominant 6-1, 6-1 victory.

I listen as Tio continues talking to the elderly man next to him, who sports a nifty blue seersucker blazer over green tennis shorts.

"We play you tomorrow in the doubles finals," Tio says.

"No, I don't think so. I'm a lot older than you."

Tio looks back at him, small gray streaks in his full head of black hair, and says, "Well, I'm 92." The seersucker guy looks back at Tio in disbelief. Then Tio serves his ace: "I know we play you."

The seersucker man seems to fade for a moment as the news settles in. Then the sparkle returns, matching his stylish dress.

Tio's doubles partner, who looks spry himself at 96, takes an empty seat at the table. The doubles partner of the seersucker guy also sits down with the group. The two doubles teams that will compete for the 90-and-over national title begin an animated conversation.

The topics range from World War II experiences in the Pacific to doubles strategy on the court. Take my 71 years out of the calculation, and the average age at this table is well over 90. And everyone, including Nancy who still plays team tennis herself, can hit a serve, forehand, backhand, and volley, the basic strokes that kids learn as young as age five.

I remember my dad, at the age of 91, in his last months, still walking around the end of the cul de sac with his walker, singing hymns he learned as a kid and had sung through a lifetime in the Methodist Church. He left organized sports with his high school football team in tiny Ripley, Mississippi, in the early 1930s.

I watch Tio and the other three 90-plus tennis players negotiate the buffet, then the ice cream bar. No walkers needed for support here. Full plates of mashed potatoes and roast beef and salmon, building energy for their doubles' final the next day. I look at Tio and realize that my return to tennis may be my path to a long life of joy, friendships, skill, and competition. I smile as I look over at Tio digging into his ice cream sundae: *That's where I want to be when I'm 92.*

Part II

STATE QUALIFIERS FROM JACKSON

These 10 Jackson tennis players qualified yesterday to play in next week's State tourney here by either winning or finishing second in the District Six tourney Thursday. The group includes: Front (left to right)—Pat Boggan, Murrah; Floyd Sulser, Ronnie Johnson, Bill Hester of Provine and Patricia Bradley of Murrah. Back—Robert Guyton, John Cutcher, Anne Burwell, Albert Simmons and Bill Finger of Murrah.—Staff Photo by Phil Wallace.

8

Loneliness
and Happiness

In the spring of 2019, I fly to Jackson, Mississippi, for the Southern Senior Men's Clay Court Open tennis championships, 70-and-over division. "Welcome to the Jackson – Medgar Wiley Evers International Airport," the sign reads as I walk off the plane. In 1963, Medgar Evers, head of the Mississippi NAACP, was assassinated in his driveway in Jackson. I was 16 that year, living across town. Like virtually all white kids in the city at the time, I knew little, if anything, about his life and death. My second season in senior tournament tennis is at hand.

I drive into the city, exiting Interstate 55 at Fortification Street, where I used to roll newspapers in a covered front porch before delivering them in the neighborhood. Driving through my old haunts, I slow the rental KIA to avoid wrecking the alignment on potholes, which seem to be everywhere. The houses and yards are weathered, a tired version of the perky streets where I rode my bike and walked to grade school more than a half century ago.

On Pinehurst Street, I pause in front of Eudora Welty's old house, now a tourist site for one of Mississippi's most celebrated authors. This native white Mississippi writer knew how to tell the truth about her state. But I only learned of

Eudora's wisdom as an adult. At the end of the block comes North State Street, the once handsome drive we took from the northern edges of Jackson into downtown landmarks: the state Capitol and Governor's mansion, the large downtown white Protestant churches, and Central High School, where I competed in high school basketball. Fond childhood images are competing with my growing sensitivity to the white privilege I knew as a kid, how white supremacy and segregation helped shape my childhood.

A few blocks away is Millsaps College. I park and then walk past the library and student union towards the old tennis courts. I look forward to seeing the house where I grew up, kindergarten through the 11th grade: the college president's home.

Young and Old

"Hi, looks like you're heading to the courts," I say to a young man with two racket handles sticking out of his backpack.

"Yeah, just going to hit a few." He smiles, his cherubic face reminds me of how I must have looked as a young college player.

"Are you on the Millsaps team?"

"Yes, I am." He beams. "The season is over now though."

"What kind of year did you guys have?" He tells me of their successes, reaching the conference semi-finals.

"I've just been over to your new facility," I say. "Well, it's new to me. I hit my first tennis balls on the old courts right over there where the gym is now. You never saw those." I point to the beautiful dome-shaped athletic building, proportionately modest for a small liberal arts school while impressive enough to attract student athletes.

"Really. Neat. No, those courts were long gone when I got here a couple of years ago."

"Do you like the new set up?" The six hard courts are divided into groups of two, giving each pair an intimacy and containment for a match.

"Yeah, it's great, with the clubhouse, the second-floor balcony so you can watch several matches at once."

We chat more about our respective tennis games and wish each other well. His season is over and yet he goes to practice his sport. I smile, picturing my drive away from Duke University after my senior year. I had tucked my Jack Kramer wood racket in the back of my red VW bug. No more school matches to play, but I was always ready to find a court for the game I loved.

As the young tennis player walks away through the small football stadium, I close my eyes and picture my early tennis strokes on the courts now gone the way of progress. The picture of a scrawny little nine-year-old gradually becomes clear. In this time capsule, another person stood on the old courts as well.

The ancient Dr. White was saying something across the net. "Watch the ball," he advised this little kid. White wisps of hair curved around his ears; funny dark blemishes dotted his otherwise bare head. I was a skinny little guy with my wooden racket, an ancient cousin of the modern versions in the tennis bag I bring to Jackson for the tournament, now at age 72.

As a kid, I managed to hit shots back to Dr. White. Then he would turn his torso, long white pants bending slightly at the knee, and punch a forehand again in my direction. Maybe he was 80 or maybe 90. I never thought about his age then. I was focusing on the next shot. I was a gutsy opponent with a knack for connecting with the ball and sending it back. Dr. White knew I was the President's son but cared little about the cute little boy with arms and legs as thin as the net posts. He concentrated on his own thin legs, moving enough to launch one more shot.

There we stood, young and old, yin and yang. The promise

of a life and the setting of the sun. What anchored these two human beings was not a rich man's sport, no country club culture, but rather some spiritual message that crossed over the taut weave of netting separating us. Some unspoken beauty sounded aloud with the twangs of ball against the mesh of nylon. The sound waves burrowed into my body deeper than any marks left by the Sunday morning ritual at downtown Galloway Methodist Church, reciting the Lord's Prayer and the Apostle's Creed with only white people. If segregated religion bred hypocrisy and confusion in me, tennis nurtured safety and joy.

Maybe thoughts of Galloway Church snap me back to the year 2019, standing here on the edge of the athletic fields at Millsaps. *I am becoming Dr. White*, I think. No long pants yet, and I can still cover the court with nimble legs.

My Closest Friend

I walk up the hill to the patio of my old house, as I did so many times, from the old Millsaps tennis courts. Mother's rose bushes are long gone. But the red-brick walls seem solid some 75 years after they were first constructed. On the same backdoor we used for everyday family traffic, a small sign reads "English Department." I open the door and turn left, up a few steps and then into our old kitchen. The stove looks the same, as does the ceramic sink. The pungent smell of cigarette smoke wafts across more than 50 years. Our maid, Katie, in white uniform, could have been sitting beside the stove, resting her feet and smoking – cooking, cleaning, and laundry done for the day.

I turn toward the dining room and see an earnest young man sorting papers on a table not nearly as elegant as the setting for our mid-day fried chicken dinners on most Saturdays. It was our "Sunday" dinner, since my dad was always away on

Sunday preaching for the Methodist-supported college.

"Hello," I say. "The door was open. Hope I'm not disturbing you."

"No problem. What brings you to the English Department?" The young man's eyes show the kind of energy and curiosity that one would hope to find at a top-notch small college.

"Well, you probably won't believe it." I pause before jumping to my purpose. "I grew up in this house. My father was president back in the 50s and early 60s. I wonder if I could look around a little."

Michael Pickard, an assistant professor of English, lays his papers aside. He seems eager to engage this gray-haired relic of an earlier age. "Of course. I've got a few minutes."

"Since we left Jackson in 1964, I've seen our house once," I say. He nods as he stands and moves toward our old living room. It appears to function even today as a central gathering spot, no new walls built for offices. "We came back, my parents and the three kids in 1989. That year, Millsaps got the first Phi Beta Kappa chapter in Mississippi. My mother represented Agnes Scott, where she was Phi Beta Kappa. And Dad was alumnus of the year."

He perks up more with that information. "I came to Millsaps as an undergraduate. And my mother also went to Agnes Scott." We smile at our common ground, even though some 30 years or so separate us. "And my father was a Methodist minister in Alabama." As he names our shared institutions in the deep South, where he has stayed and I have rarely visited, we turn into what had been my parents' bedroom. The college carved it into two offices and took away the old bathroom. But I can still picture my mother asleep on Sunday afternoons on the big oak bed that came from my grandmother's house. She was exhausted from being the president's wife and raising three young children, beginning at ages eight, five, and one when we moved here in 1952.

We peek into the den with the shelves that held the dark

red Encyclopedia Britannica volumes. The couch where Dad often took a nap on Saturday afternoons, after a morning at the office, has gone the way of time. My host is about to turn back to my parents' old bedroom when I eye the door to the side yard. Again, a time warp guides my heart and mind.

A gangly pimple-faced teenager, I was opening the door. A young man stood in front of me, visibly nervous. He asked politely if President Finger was home. "I think he's at the Christian Center," I answered, then watched him walk up the winding sidewalk away from the house. He was probably the first Negro I had ever seen face-to-face in a coat and tie.

Many years later, Dad told me that the young man was with a group of students from Tougaloo College. This historically African American school just north of Jackson functioned at the center of many civil rights activities. The students wanted President Finger to support their efforts to integrate the Christian Center, the building used by Millsaps for chapel services, the annual performance of the Messiah, and other sacred occasions. This college centerpiece took its name after a faith guided by a singular phrase: "love your neighbor as yourself."

As that awkward teenager image floats away, Dr. Pickard and I move down the small hall beside my parents' old closet towards the kids' rooms. My host works out of my sister's old bedroom. Framed images look down from the walls like a fresh coat of paint. Two large black and white photos of an aging Eudora Welty suggest the wisdom she carried. Beside the portraits is my host's PhD diploma from the University of Virginia. He follows my eyes across his wall and offers, "I teach American literature, including Mississippi writers."

The bathroom between my sister's room and the room I shared with my brother still has the pink tile sink and large built-in bathtub. The chairman of the department is at work in my old room, so we do not see the site of my old desk or bed next to the kitchen. The house feels like an old friend, like family. This place was my closest friend for 12 years, a time that witnessed in Mississippi and across the country a second American revolution, this one based on race.

I have taken enough of his time and head out the way I came, through the kitchen. The patio looks small now. How did I ever hit so many tennis balls against the garage door? How could I hear my mother's dinner bell as she stood here looking toward the old tennis courts?

The Power of Joy

As a boy, I would often hit serves alone on the two lower courts, just across the football field. Standing at the baseline, to the right of the hash mark in the middle, I would aim diagonally to the deuce court. My left hand tossed the ball two or three feet above my head as I bent my knees and cocked my sinew of a body like a spring. Then I reached up from my five-foot frame to smack the ball from the highest point my racket could muster. When I connected perfectly with the floating ball, I felt the promise of more. More power, more grace, more hope. More alive in the world than I felt anywhere else.

The power of joy passed through me, and I wanted more. I reached down into the blue jean bag tied to my waist, another ball at the ready. Then another, going for the service box again and again. My mother had sensed that tennis held some fascination for me and had fashioned this ball bag from a leg of some worn out blue jeans. It held about 15 balls. I found abandoned balls around the Millsaps courts and filled it for practicing.

With my bag empty, balls were scattered around the far side of the court with a few in the net as well. I would walk around the net post, gather the balls into my bag, find the hash mark at the middle of the other baseline and do it all again ... and again ... and again. I loved my old blue jean ball bag. Finally, I would hear my mother's dinner bell. Reluctantly gathering the last balls, I walked down the hill from the courts, across 40 yards of the football field, and scurried past one of the goalposts up a hill to our patio. In the garage, I tightened the screws on the press that kept the wood frame from warping.

As a young lad, I tried my hand at most sports. My dad found time to throw baseballs with me when I was young and later came to some of my football and basketball games. I enjoyed these team sports but felt a singular pull onto the tennis court, some different kind of magic. Alone, away from family rhythms, racial preoccupations, and daily life. Neither my dad nor mom ever saw me play a tournament tennis match, and that was fine with me. Tennis was my domain.

My parents, both native Mississippians and liberal thinkers, decided to raise a family in their home state, a place they loved despite the legacies of white supremacy. Many Methodist ministers left the state when the Civil Rights revolution came, but Mother and Dad decided to stay. At Millsaps, my parents did not bring the pressures they felt into family conversations. Nor did schoolteachers in our all-white classes address race, not once throughout the years.

Still the family often watched the national evening news together in the den, usually CBS with Douglas Edwards and later Walter Cronkite. The *Clarion Ledger*, then one of the most conservative papers in the country, did cover the major civil rights events in the state but with its slant. I saw the headlines as I rolled newspapers with my brother for early morning deliveries. When we went to Jackson for the Phi Beta Kappa weekend in 1989, at age 41, I learned more.

On that trip, Dad, Mother, and I visited the college archives in the Millsaps library. From President Finger papers, 1952-1964, Dad pulled out a box from 1958 labeled "Integration." My mother spotted the scrapbook she had made of newspaper clippings on one of the signature events during his presidency.

On a Friday afternoon in the spring of 1958, the head of the Jackson Citizens' Council, the white-collar supporter of the Ku Klux Klan, walked past my father's secretary and stormed into his office. He handed my father an envelope and demanded that he immediately read the letter. Instead, Dad asked him to leave, put the letter into his desk, unopened, and told the intruder that he answered to the Board of Trustees of the College, not to him.

Dad left his office in Murrah Hall and walked across the street, down the long driveway past the side of the Science Building to our patio. I was waiting with two gloves and a baseball. He loosened his tie, took off his coat, and put on the glove I handed to him. Then we played catch. I was 11, he was 41.

On Monday, back in his office, Dad read the letter. "The Citizens' Councils and patriotic public officials are engaged in a life and death struggle," it said. "It is intolerable for Millsaps College, right here in the heart of Mississippi, to be in the apparent position of undermining everything we are fighting for." The letter concluded: "I tell you frankly and without rancor that the time has come for a showdown. Either you and your faculty are for segregation, or you are for integration. In the best interests of the college, will you make known which position you and every member of your faculty support?" The letter made its way into the press.

Notes came to Dad from rural Mississippi towns with names I heard throughout my childhood – Tupelo and Iuka and Pontotoc, some of the towns where Dad would drive and preach every Sunday morning promoting the college, while Mother got us off to church. The Methodist churches throughout the state were the main funding source for the college in that era. "We, the undersigned members of the Official Board of the Coffeeville Methodist Church, in our monthly session this night wish to express our confidence in your leadership ability as President of Millsaps College," read one. Twelve scrawling signatures followed. Churches across the state supported Dad's position: to answer to the Board of Trustees, not to the Citizens' Council. In Mississippi in 1958, standing up to the Citizens' Council was the closest white churches – and my father – could come to supporting integration publicly.

I did know something was terribly wrong in Jackson, even when I first found the Millsaps tennis courts as a boy. The Citizens' Council defined the principle in the world around me in their mission statement: "the maintenance of segregation by all legal and legitimate means." My childhood psyche felt disconnected from the world outside the safety of my family. At home and at church, the two nurturing institutions in my life, I could not reconcile the fallacy: I was guided by a religion where God loves everybody but would only let some of His children come into our place of worship and into the rooms where I learned my ABCs.

My formative, cellular-level memory absorbed images of African Americans as servants for Whites – as maids, yard-men, farm hands, gas station assistants. I saw only white class-mates and tennis buddies, only white teachers, only white preachers and doctors and professors. We sang a favorite song at the breakfast table, "In Christ there is no East or West, in Him no North or South." But these words always rang hollow. The first black person I knew as an equal was another student at Duke University.

I went to the tennis courts as a place of refuge from a confusing world, a place of psychological rest. If loneliness took me to the tennis courts, then happiness kept me there.

9

Magic at Work

By 1960, at age 12 and in the seventh grade, I was a pretty good little tennis player. My brother and I played at the Millsaps courts, and I was gradually finding a few other kids who loved tennis, mostly at Battlefield Park across town, with its beautiful green-clay rubico courts. My mother was often too busy to take me to Battlefield, so I sometimes rode the bus, boarding it on Northwest Street near our house at Millsaps College.

When the big, noisy bus made its downtown stops, lots of black people got on and headed to the back of the bus. I was thinking about tennis as the bus meandered through the town toward the Battlefield Park stop. Tennis was the propelling engine for me – hearing the thump of the ball against the strings, running down a drop shot, learning to hit a volley and a forehand with power. I must have noticed the color of the people around me, but the contradictions in my world did not command my attention. Instead, the impact of segregation lodged somewhere in my body, unattended, waiting to be discovered and understood.

When I got off the bus, I went to the tennis clubhouse where Dorothy Vest ruled like a kind den mother. She directed kids to courts, signed people up for lessons, and promoted tournaments here and in other cities. Her glasses fell down her nose as she looked up from one of her tournament draw sheets to see me. She had strong, athletic legs, dark hair, and penetrating serious eyes. She knew all the kids' names and how serious we were about tennis. Her husband, a bit older, would teach lessons. Their youngest child still played at the park, with strokes as smooth as silk.

"You and Erskine can play on the rubico today, the end court," she said. Erskine, a year younger than me, had come with his father. We often played together here and sometimes on our side of town as well. The public tennis center had a row of six, well-manicured composition courts and some hard-surfaced courts. With the rat-a-tat sounds of balls from the always active courts, this corner of the sprawling Battlefield Park sounded like friendly combat, with rackets as our weapons.

"I won't charge you for the court," she would say to me and Erskine, "so long as you practice at least 30 minutes before you play a set." She knew we wanted to just go out and play to see who could win. She also knew better than we did the value that drills would have on our developing games. "First, hit cross-court forehands and then backhands," she said. "Keep the ball behind the service line. Then you can practice down the line – backhand for one and forehand for the other."

We would then happily head to the last court in the row, with paying players in the closer courts, to start our practice. We were an even match. We were friends with our rackets – we helped each other get better. When we played, neither of us could imagine being anywhere else. We were two happy kids, forgetting about our town, our school, even our families. We just hit the ball.

Some days, before we played, Erskine would get a lesson. His father, a lawyer who played in a weekly doubles game on the composition courts, saw the value in lessons for his son's promising game. Mrs. Vest would send Erskine out with her husband as the instructor. I would walk to the bleachers that overlooked the dark-green courts, sit in the stands, and listen to what Mr. Vest told Erskine.

"Your feet and your eyes are the most important parts of your body for tennis," he would say. He talked about footwork, keeping your eye on the ball, and being aware of your opponent's position. I soaked it all in. The Vests did not mind me getting what amounted to a free lesson, as I sat beside this sea of green with words of wisdom seeping into my psyche. I do not recall ever asking my parents to pay for lessons. I knew there was little extra money.

At Battlefield, I had a growing sense of promise, of hope, which had begun with my serves on the Millsaps courts. Mrs. Vest noticed me, which made me feel like I belonged to something bigger than my fledgling game. The tradition of public tennis courts was marching across the country on the backs of dedicated servants of the game like Dorothy Vest. But even she could not take the country-club sport too far into the general domain. No black players at Battlefield Park in the 1950s and 1960s. In the South, the chances of a black player rising beyond playground level would be virtually impossible. Yet, Arthur Ashe did it, from playing first with other black kids in Brook Field in Richmond, Virginia, then with his father's help, finding his way to selected mentors, where he climbed the improbable ladder to become a Wimbledon champion.

Mr. Clean and the Kid

During the summer of 1960, Erskine would join other kids whom Mrs. Vest organized for tournaments around Jackson. But I was not part of this group. Throughout my childhood, our family spent most of each summer across the South in the North Carolina mountains at Lake Junaluska, home of the Southeastern Conference Methodist Assembly.

The family looked forward to our time in what became a kind of paradise for us kids, away from the stifling summer heat and oppressive racial tensions of Mississippi. We could swim and play all types of sports at the athletic fields, explore mountain streams, and, over the years, build a permanent set of summer friends – many of them other Methodist ministers' kids. I would pick up tennis games as often as possible on one of the two concrete courts at the Lake, but I missed the tournaments, where kids' games got better.

Sometimes, during that summer of 1960, I would see Mr. Martin, the manager of the swimming pool, head across the parking lot toward the tennis courts. In his loose tennis shorts and oversized white t-shirt, he moved gracefully for such a huge man. In two large strides, he was over the narrow strip of grass that bordered the two concrete courts. Here a stray forehand could send the ball over the fence onto the volleyball court, rolling toward the swimming pool.

Mr. Martin had a small head, bald crown, and bushy eyebrows to go with his massive frame. He resembled the then-familiar icon, Mr. Clean. He liked to play with diminutive Johnny Stokes, maybe 5 feet 8, a college student. Stokes always looked immaculate in crisp white togs, with a towel folded into his shorts to wipe away the sweat between points. Mr. Martin was not a polished player like Johnny Stokes, but he had power. One afternoon, I was delighted to hear Stokes say he had to leave early.

"Can I hit a few with you?" I asked Mr. Clean. A rising eighth grader now, I weighed in at the most 110 pounds to Mr. Martin's bulk, let's call it 275.

"Sure, hop on the court."

Mr. Martin knew me from the four summers he had managed the swimming pool at Lake Junaluska. With my buddies at the Lake, from an early age, I had taken early morning lessons in the freezing cold swimming pool. The water was as dark as the lake outside the stone wall that separated the pool from the lake.

That afternoon, when I stepped onto the court with Mr. Martin, I had recently finished the Red Cross Junior Life

Saving course. In my final test, I had "rescued" Mr. Martin. My little arm could barely reach half-way over his barrel chest. But I put everything I had into my scissors kick and held on tight as I pulled the water back with my right arm and "saved" Mr. Martin, getting him to the edge of the pool.

A tennis court, whether in Jackson or Lake Junaluska, felt like home. I knew I could hit the ball. Still, when he served, nervousness edged over to fear. Mr. Clean tilted his bald head and gazed skyward, sent the toss up from his massive left forearm, and arched his racket to make the explosive connection in the crisp mountain air. The tennis racket and ball looked too delicate for his mass of muscle. But something about the graceful game of tennis tied together the disparate image.

At first, I tried returning his power by standing at the back edge of the four feet of concrete behind the baseline of the court. But the ball would whiz past before I could even swing my racket. Mr. Martin knew I could play and did not make it easy for me. I learned gradually that to be able to get a good swing, I needed to step back even more, off the concrete surface behind the baseline. I finally moved all the way to the edge of grass and dirt next to the tall link-chain fence that separated us from the volleyball court.

I stood there, a waif grasping my Kramer on common ground with this huge adult. He was away from his school-year teaching job, and I was far from the familiar games with Erskine at Battlefield Park. But here we were. The court was our equalizer, not in the quality of our game but in our state of mind. We were sharing this space. The rules stood for all tennis courts, rubico or concrete. We each had to place the serve in the same box diagonally away from the starting position at the baseline. But also present were the particularities of this court, this place, this moment in time. My small, skinny body, just edging into adolescence, eyes alive with the drama of the moment, stood toe to toe with massive Wallace Martin. I could hit his serve back and won a few points.

The rules of the game transcended the place. Hit the serve back over the net. Win a point. My objective was not to defeat an opponent. It was to feel competent and, beyond that, joy. Part of that pleasure came from being noticed by Mr. Martin. He took me as a worthy partner in this sacred space of sport. And I did my part, focusing, playing as best I could, appreciating his kindness. Meanwhile, something beyond either of us played itself out. For such joy to occur, some magic was at work in this singular moment on earth. I found a way to belong.

A Tiger by the Tail

Back in Jackson for the school year, including the spring tennis seasons, I played on our junior high team and in the city tournaments that Mrs. Vest organized on the Battlefield Courts. She organized these just after school was over, so more people could play before going on vacation. In junior high school, Erskine was a year behind me, so I would play the top player in the other schools. The problem came when we played Peoples Junior High because Bill Hester was their best player.

Bill Hester moved through the Battlefield Park stream of talented tennis players nurtured by Dorothy Vest. His father, a notable tennis player himself and later president of the U.S. Tennis Association, dressed little six-year-old Bill in all whites and sent him onto the Battlefield courts for lessons from the Vests. In middle school, Hester, in his crisp tennis whites, had an imposing presence. His wardrobe included a neatly folded towel tucked into the right side of his shorts, like Johnny Stokes at Lake Junaluska, where he could wipe sweat off his right hand before a point. He seemed quiet off the court. Once the match started, he focused entirely on the tennis ball.

My ninth-grade year, age 15, I thought I might have a

chance to beat Hester. I was getting better and more confident. The problem was, he was better too. In our junior high school match, I lost 6-0, 6-0, my only such drubbing as a kid. I walked off the hard courts, shocked and embarrassed. "You had a tiger by the tail today," the coach said. I felt a little better. We both knew he was right – that tiger was out of my league, at least that day.

Despite sustaining the worst loss of my young tennis life, I was determined to get better. Then, I had a breakthrough in the early summer city tournament before we left for Lake Junaluska. I played in the 15 and under division and, at Mrs. Vest's encouragement, entered the next category up, the 18 and under. I played Hester in a much closer match in the finals of the 15 and under division, but my real joy came in beating one of my older brother's high school tennis teammates in the 18s. A great sendoff for another summer at Lake Junaluska.

10

Tacos and Potholes

The drive from Millsaps College to the River Hills Tennis Club takes about 10 minutes, past the sprawling University of Mississippi Medical Center. After passing Murrah High School, where I played on the basketball and tennis teams, I reach what looks like a small country club. I step into a large foyer and then a dining room, where men in suits are laying materials on tables for some kind of meeting. This does not look like my tennis club at home, where a person is usually stringing a racket just inside the entrance.

"Do you know where the tennis courts are?" I ask one of the men.

"Not a clue," he says.

I make my way through the dining room, empty in late afternoon, to the patio that looks out on two rows of green clay courts. A plaque on the edge of the first court honors Bill Hester's father, William "Slew" Hester, who spearheaded the creation of this club in 1964, the year I left Jackson. Slew Hester built on his experience with River Hills to undertake the much more ambitious goal of launching the U.S. Open tennis center beginning in 1977, when he was president of the U.S. Tennis Association.

Two sweaty teenagers, sitting on the patio after a match, direct me to another building toward the back of the courts. I walk between the banks of clay and hard courts to reach the large but more modest structure. A counter is piled high with clean white towels. I ask the woman at a computer if any players have arrived early for the tournament and are looking for a practice partner. She points to a list with one name. I call him.

"Sounds great," Matt Houseman says from his hotel. "I can be over in about 20 minutes."

The week before, Houseman flew to Louisiana from his home in La Quinta, California, to begin a three-week jaunt through the senior tournament schedule, first in Baton Rouge, then Jackson, and next week to Atlanta. Here we are, from the Pacific and the Atlantic, to play a tennis game. Two old guys with hopes of winning and a love of competition. Hitting a little ball with accuracy and speed across a net offers us great satisfaction, timing our swings to the complicated spins that opponents send our way. I have a new friend, a comrade seeking joy in a game contained in a rectangle 78 feet by 27 feet (for singles), a place of infinite varieties of strokes and counterpunches.

Ten years my junior, he hits the ball a lot harder than I do. Invigorated and challenged by the extra pace, I manage about 20 minutes before we take a break. "I couldn't play when I turned 60 last year because of some injuries," he says, as we wipe off the sweat and drink water. "I decided to go all in this year if I could."

"How did you manage to get three weeks away? Are you married?" I'm thinking about the planning I had to do with my wife. My trip to Jackson is a priority for this second year back to serious tennis competition.

"My wife is supportive," Houseman says. "But even after just a week, I can feel the distance. I'm getting a little lonely, especially with these days between the tournaments."

We work for another 20 minutes on serves and returns before stopping for the day. I head back to the informal tennis building and walk past four indoor courts to a modest locker room with benches and metal lockers. No carpet.

Safety in a New Mississippi Flag

On the way to the Airbnb where I will spend five nights, I pass Eastover Drive, where I played in occasional backyard baseball games behind what was then a large, avant-garde house. Still called the Eastover section, large homes remain but with a few potholes even here. As I turn down Meadowbrook, I pass newer gated communities on both sides and then cross Interstate 55 into what was the modern, middle-class suburbs of North Jackson 50 years ago.

The potholes increase as I head toward the intersection of North State Street and Meadowbrook Road, once a thriving crossroads complete with a shopping center of clothing stores and a bowling alley, the places I remember as a teenager. North State Street here is closed except for local traffic for a major renovation. A pawn shop, dollar store, and gas stations fill the intersection, along with a Piggly Wiggly that appears to be closed.

As I turn into a residential area, two short blocks away, I pass a vacant lot with large piles of brush and a sign: "No dumping of trash." I avoid several large potholes and ease into a neatly maintained driveway with a proposed new Mississippi state flag hanging from the house. On the airplane, I read that New York City had just taken the Mississippi state flag down from the 50 flags that fly at the Statue of Liberty. The official Mississippi banner has the Confederate flag in the corner. A new proposed flag has become a symbol of moderate voices in Mississippi. [The State adopted a new flag in 2021 without the Confederate flag on it.]

Beside this flag, I feel my body relax as I punch in the code the owners sent me. A woman greets me and points me to my room upstairs, where I will share a bath with guests who stay in the other upstairs room. The $41 a night lodging helps my budget for the trip.

"Everything looks fine and clear," I say, back downstairs.

Her husband, who looks about 28 years old, is cooking something that smells delicious. "It'll take me a while to get used to Jackson now, after all these years away." On my Airbnb request, I told them I was returning to Jackson after many years to play in a senior tennis tournament. "The potholes make a big impression right away. In the old neighborhoods near Millsaps, where I used to play as a kid, they're terrible!"

"Yeah, the streets are like a third world country in many places," she says. "But we're used to it now."

"How long have you lived here, in Jackson?"

"About seven or eight years."

"What brought you here, to Mississippi?"

"Graduate school, at Mississippi Southern in Hattiesburg. Then, a job at the hospital here."

We talk a bit about places to eat in Fondren, described in the literature in my room as a bustling, dynamic area of the city not far from here. She gives me directions to avoid the closed section of North State Street. As I head out the door for dinner, I see an African American man across the street on his porch. Driving away, a nicely dressed black woman comes out of the house next door. My hosts are White. Seven minutes later, I realize that Fondren is a neighborhood I once knew.

The parking lot in front of Brent's Drugs seems unchanged and somehow manages to accommodate today's huge SUVs along with my rented KIA. I peek inside one of the last places I visited in Jackson before leaving in 1964 and see the same soda fountain. The restaurant booths and tables are packed, a welcoming group is at the entrance. A special event has the place booked, so I head across the street to what was once Duling Elementary. My Power Elementary peewee football team played Duling once upon a time. My skinny arms could spiral a pass to a precise spot, my last successes in football.

The renovated 1928 Duling School now hosts a seafood restaurant at one end and a performance area in the middle. I see crowds teeming in the parking lot on the right, next to Babalu Tapas & Tacos. On this mild early May evening, the sign outside announces, "Taco Tuesdays" with $2 tacos. I decide against a long wait for an outside table and get seated right away inside at a tall table in the row against the wall, near the kitchen and the bar.

Settled onto a back-supported stool, my high perch gives me a good view of that corner of the restaurant. I feel more tourist than native. The animated conversation between two women sitting at the bar, one White and one Black, would not have been possible in my era, except among civil rights workers gathered not so far away at Tougaloo College.

There always seemed some hope in my childlike innocence, when I tossed a baseball in our side yard with Jeannette, the daughter of our maid, Katie. One day Katie did not bring her daughter around on the Saturday when she cooked the fried chicken, and I never saw Jeannette again. We were getting too old for a little white boy to play with a little black girl in the city.

Two bartenders work shoulder to shoulder, trying to keep up with the crush of orders on this raucous Tuesday night in hip Fondren. For the moment their contrasting skin colors melt away into the energy of good food and drinks.

When my tacos arrive, I salivate for my first meal since airport food. As I revel in this new Jackson that I never thought I would see, I notice the restless young black man two tables away. He is looking at the kitchen window where waiters stream in and out. A waitress brings him a tray of tacos. He picks at his food, then gets down from the high seat and walks into the kitchen. He offers advice to one of the cooks and comes back to his plate in the dining room. He chats with the wait staff as they go by. Again, he leaves his food, walks past the back of the bar into the kitchen, appearing to sort out some issue.

My four tacos look like a lot of food until I taste how good they are. I eat too fast and look at this young man's untouched food. One empty table separates us. As he settles his lean body back into his seat, he happens to look my way. Our eyes meet.

"You seem busy," I say over the empty table. "Can't even eat your dinner."

He smiles. "I'm the sous chef here. It's a busy night." He looks about 30 years old. Speaking with the kitchen and wait staff, Black and White, he combines authority with comradeship, easygoing with businesslike.

Driving back to my Airbnb, back down Northwest Street to avoid the one-lane, rocky North State Street, I wonder what kind of job this man might have had if he had grown up when Jeannette and I did. I think about the African American men who did make their way up the old Canton Road past the side of the old Duling School to Tougaloo College, either as students or as civil rights workers. How much had that journey changed their lives?

I feel both pride and despair as I leave this pocket of hope and hip in the center of post-revolutionary Mississippi, driving through dark, uneven streets. Over the years, I have found myself from time-to-time defending Mississippi, oddly, while trying to sort out my guilt as a white liberal southerner.

On a vacation visiting with my wife's sister in California, my Mississippi roots came up. I was telling these liberals on the west coast about an interview with an African American professor on a local talk show on National Public Radio. She described being nervous on a car trip with a group going into Mississippi to help with a post-Katrina project. When the group walked into a restaurant in rural southern Mississippi, the place grew totally silent. All eyes went to the interracial group. The group's leader announced to the silent customers that they were heading south to help rebuild. Without hesitation, everyone in the restaurant stood and applauded. I found myself choking up on the final phrases of the story, filled with pride and hope for my homeland.

Public Court Tennis Legacy

The directions to Carol Ann Vest's house in Ridgeland, just north of Jackson, take me past the potholes on Meadowbrook to I-55. The interstate corridor sends commuters and tennis players to Jackson from suburbs with well-paved streets filled with Whole Foods, Target, and other national chains. The route surprises me when I turn onto the Natchez Trace Parkway. This scenic drive with low speed limits stretches diagonally from the southwest edge of the state into Tennessee. As a kid, after we had "Santa Claus" in the living room at Millsaps, we made the long, slow trip via the Natchez Trace to Ripley, near the Tennessee border, where my father grew up, and our relatives waited for us for Christmas dinner.

Today, while no family occasion awaits me, I hope for a trove of tennis memories and stories. The oldest of Dorothy Vest's three children, Carol Ann, is working in her front yard when I arrive. This 79-year-old, can-do woman, who still plays tennis regularly, is moving paving stones beside her driveway. She has recently moved back to Jackson, where she lived for many years, from Texas, where she cared for her aging mother. We had several phone calls in recent months about my book project and my connection to her mother.

"I'm going to have to get someone out here to help me," she says, pointing to the holes she dug beside her driveway, each a bit deeper moving down the slope. The street looks like any other quiet middle-class neighborhood in suburban America.

Inside, U.S. Senate hearings are playing on the small TV in her breakfast room, as the U.S. Attorney General fields questions before a captive American audience on Special Counsel Robert Mueller's report. "That Lindsay Graham is an idiot," she grumbles as she turns the hearings off. No alternative Mississippi flag hangs from her home, but I realize I stepped into another home of emotional safety.

After a glass of water and a few short memories of her mother and Battlefield Park, she says, "The best thing is for you to come in and see my tennis museum." For more than an hour, Carol Ann flips through scrapbooks of the family's tennis adventures and explains the photos and mementos on the walls, interspersing details with the story of her mother's and her own life.

If Dorothy Vest had not found her way to the public courts in Jackson, Mississippi, tennis would not have been a serious part of my life. I think of Dorothy Vest as one of my heroes. Her tennis story began in Texas. "My father taught high school math in Brownsville, Texas, at the very tip of Texas," Carol Ann Vest tells me during our visit at her house in 2019. "He persuaded my mother, who was in his high school class, to play on the school tennis team."

John Vest, 13 years older than his high school pupil, eventually married Dorothy and brought her back to his native Mississippi. An eccentric man, he liked math and building things, and held a variety of jobs, including building the Battlefield Park courts. But he never stayed with a job long, and gradually Dorothy became the main family bread winner, primarily with a 30-year career as the City of Jackson tennis director.

They had three kids to support. Carol Ann, the oldest, and her brother Allen became good players, but it was the youngest, Becky, who reached international levels, eventually playing with the likes of Billie Jean King. "But there wasn't enough money in women's tennis in those days," Carol Ann says, "So Becky didn't stay with it long."

Carol Ann remembers when her mother started to work. "She hired maids to take care of us." This shift in the household led Carol Ann to see a broader view of her town.

"One day I was riding a bus and watched a black woman get on. I could tell she was tired from working all day. She sat in one of the few seats left, just behind the sign that ended the whites only section. At another stop, a white teenager got on and walked up to where she sat and said he wanted that seat. So, the bus driver got up and moved the sign back one row. Then the woman had to stand up since no seat was available, and the white boy took her seat. I went up to the driver and said that wasn't right, the woman had been sitting behind the sign. He told me to get off the bus and never ride his bus again. If I did, I would be in big trouble. He was mean, frightening to a little girl."

That incident made a big impression on Carol Ann. After college at nearby Belhaven College, she went to Brazil in the Peace Corps. When she came back, now the mid-1960s, she moved back in with her parents while she volunteered with civil rights groups and attended events at Tougaloo College, the hub of the famous "Freedom Summer" of 1964. Her parents began to get threats about her being at their home. "It was time for me to move out anyway, so I went off on my own." Later, as a young woman, she worked for a year at the U.S. Office of Equal Opportunity.

Carol Ann surprises me as the conversation turns to the ever-charged issue of race. I'm not sure how to pursue that angle of our conversation. "I thought of your mother as a great example of public court tennis," I say, "working with anyone who had the commitment to get better, regardless of how much money a family might have. But I assume she couldn't help black kids in those days."

"Not at Battlefield, everything was segregated." But she did have an opportunity to be a pioneer, Carol Ann is quick to add. "It was 1966, I think, when she sponsored the Southern all-star girls' team. Becky was on it, and one African American girl from North Carolina, Bonnie Logan." Mrs. Vest put Logan on the team over protests from some of the Southern Tennis Association leaders, Carol Ann recalls.

Mrs. Vest drove the team to the national competition, being held in Philadelphia. "The club would not let the black girl stay in the designated housing with the other players. My mother said she is staying with our team, regardless of what the club says, and she'll room with my daughter. The next day," Carol Ann says, "the club actually tried to block Bonnie's entrance, but my mother didn't let them."

In her later years, Mrs. Vest left Battlefield and moved to a new city facility in North Jackson, where Carol Ann, as head pro, helped her organize lessons and tournaments. Aware that the city was paying Mrs. Vest less than men in a comparable position in the recreation department, she sued based on sex discrimination, long before such a term was commonplace. She eventually won a modest settlement, Carol Ann says. In that new job, she also helped with desegregation, Carol Ann says. She welcomed all black players, made them feel welcome, and had family parties at the courts. "I made sure they were invited and committed to bringing a dish!" adds Carol Ann.

Mrs. Vest found time to play tennis herself. "Slew Hester loved to play hard doubles games at Battlefield," Carol Ann says. "He got my mother to play with his group; she was the best player around for them. She would always come home with bruises where one of the guys had hit her with a volley."

When Mrs. Vest retired, she returned to Texas, and Carol Ann moved to support her in her final years. Dorothy Vest, who died at the age of 93 in 2013, was elected to the Mississippi Tennis Hall of Fame, the Southern Tennis Hall of Fame, and the Mississippi Sports Hall of Fame. In 1979, the Vests were the USTA Tennis Family of the Year.

Her love for tennis and nurturing kids like me contributed to her long life, Carol Ann believes. "Tennis keeps us healthy, physically and mentally," she says, citing the recent research from Europe where tennis players lived longer than other athletes doing solo sports, such as cycling and jogging. "The social aspect is so important," Carol Ann says.

Carol Ann moved back to Jackson after her mother died. She has a new group of friends at a nearby tennis club. "But I hurt my shoulder and will have to have surgery. I used to play doubles in the morning, then have lunch, and have plenty of interaction with people. Now that I can't play, I can get depressed. I come back to my house by myself and miss the social contact."

Walking me to my car on the street, she talks about the neighborhood. "I like it here. I could complain that some people don't take care of their lawns, but it's pretty nice. A lot of black families live here. There's black flight from Jackson as well as white."

● 11 ●

Finding My Landing Spot

In 1963, the spring of my sophomore year at Murrah High School, our tennis team had solid players in four of the five events: boys' singles and doubles, girls' doubles, and mixed doubles. The District 6 tournament would determine who would qualify for the state tournament. My game had improved since junior high. I was eager to play Bill Hester, the favorite for the district and state championship. He and I moved through our early rounds without incident. For the district championship, the boys' singles match was the premier event, so Mrs. Vest put us on the court closest to the club house.

As the first set unfolded, the score stayed close. We matched shot for shot – the best I had ever played against him. With a final burst of winners and a few uncharacteristic mistakes from Hester, I eked out the first set, seven games to five. But he had seen enough and went to work. He picked up momentum in the second set, winning 6-2, before skunking me 6-0 to win the best two out of three sets. Despite my loss, our team took the district championship, winning the mixed doubles and the runner-up spots in my singles category, along with boys' doubles and girls' doubles.

A newspaper photo shows the Jackson players going to the state tournament. Hester looks relaxed with a slight smile, kneeling near the right end of the first row, no erect back like those beside him. In contrast, I stand in the back row expressionless, a hard-to-read face, unsure of who I am on the court and off. I hold my wooden racket like a security blanket. My face looks like a mask, hardened, distant from the moment. The image seems to obscure more pain than just losing a match.

Looking at the clipping now, I think of another photo, when I was four, from the 1951 family Christmas card. In that posed shot on the parsonage steps in Oxford, Mississippi, before we moved to Jackson, I sit at the right, my brother, age seven, at the left. Our sister, almost one, sits in the center with the innocent smile of an infant. This photo was taken just months after my mother's postpartum break-down and hospital treatment. Working in midlife to understand my own cycles of depression, I found this photo of my four-year-old self, blew it up and put it over my desk. As I wrote about depression and the ways I was moving through it, I sent love and compassion to the little kid who surely still lived inside of me.

Now in my 70s, back in Jackson for the tournament, I look closely again at the photo of me at age 16. Where is the big smile I earned after taking a set from the best player around and heading to the state tournament? This 16-year-old – looking out from a crinkled newspaper clipping of successful tennis players – seems to hold more promise than the four-year-old. By age 16, I am part of a tribe, moving through the district tournament and onto the state championships, and further. My thin, taut face captures traces of both the belonging and the isolation that I felt that spring in Jackson.

Summer of 1963

In early June, because of a summer job, I left for Lake Junaluska before the family. My dad took me to the Greyhound Bus Station just blocks from the State Capitol. While I was vaguely aware that the Freedom Riders had come to this very bus station, I was focused on my own adventure. I boarded my overnight bus ride, riding alone to Nashville, Tennessee, where my aunt met me. She took me to her apartment for a huge breakfast and then took me back for a second overnight bus ride through the North Carolina mountains to my job at the Lake Junaluska cafeteria.

Two tiny cabins stuffed with bunk beds and a simple bathroom were home for me and the other eight guys who served food and washed dishes. My annual search among the current Junaluska staffers led me to possible tennis partners. But there were no dedicated players like Bill Hester or Erskine Wells, who were spending their days on the Battlefield courts and playing summer tournaments. While I missed the excitement and comradery of tennis tournaments, I was glad to be away from the Mississippi heat and racial tensions simmering through the city. The summer days passed quickly, living and working with friends, playing volleyball and tennis and ping pong between duties at the cafeteria, and taking outings in the mountains.

On Saturday nights, many of us would head to a large square dance barn in nearby Maggie Valley. We summer visitors joined with locals to promenade and buck dance before a caller in overalls with his sidekicks playing dobro and guitar, fiddle and bass. I loved the sense of abandonment, whether swinging about with 200-pound mountain women or wispy seven-year-old girls. The buck dancing brought out my best footwork in showmanship clogging, a driving, rhythmic tapping and shuffling of feet. Whether clogging improved my footwork on the tennis court, who could say. But I loved every minute on that square dance floor. Clogging, like tennis, took me into my body, far away from the complexities of the world. No pressure of Mississippi racism, no unconscious absorption of white privilege.

On a Sunday afternoon outing, I had the same out-of-mind joyfulness. I had to use the same quick feet needed for hard-driving clogging or hard-to-reach tennis shots. About six cars made a 45-minute drive into the Smokey Mountains, parking within earshot of a huge stream rumbling down the mountain. We called the adventure "rock hopping." No formal race or competition, no score like a tennis match, just teenagers and young college guys and gals jumping into the elements.

First-timers, less athletic souls, and cautious ones headed onto the first boulder near the road. A few stood up hesitantly and tried a short jump to an adjacent completely dry rock, far enough away from the water to avoid any danger of slipping. I joined the more adventurous group. Would I pause completely and examine my next option for safety, my next boulder, or move in steady motion trusting my feet to find a dry enough landing spot? I would have to make choices again and again, as I followed the roaring water around and over the huge slabs of stone before me.

That afternoon in the deafening roar, I could not hear Paul Finney ahead of me but could see him point to tricky spots between us. My agility had been sharpened over the years through repeated starts and stops on tennis and basketball courts. But Finney was on a higher level, floating from rock to rock, his feet groomed from years of soccer in India where he grew up.

I watched as he jumped off a massive rock into the air but saw no landing spot. In mid-air, he pivoted his body to the left where he found solid rock. He hardly broke stride as he leaned forward, heading down his rock path beside the gushing water. I felt the danger and slowed down, knowing I was not in his league. Finney was three years older with instincts in his feet far more developed than mine. I stopped and found a new route, preparing for another section where I could pick up the pace.

On those rocks, joy coursed through me, a message from the elements. I felt totally alive, with the mist and roar of water all about me. The giant boulders offered my only way home, my choices of steps, my anchors, my guide through the clouds of steam around me.

Louisiana Open

When we returned to Jackson in late August, just before my junior year of high school, I headed to Battlefield Park to play serious tennis again. "Bill, there's a tournament coming up that would be a good fit for you," Mrs. Vest told me. The Louisiana Open Junior Tournament was coming up in Shreveport, several hundred miles west of Jackson. "I can work out a ride for you and housing. Check with your parents to see if you can go."

Unlike today, no kids packed piles of rackets in long Wilson or Prince racket bags. A few might have two wooden rackets. I took my single Jack Kramer, wore my only pair of sneakers, and packed my white shorts and shirts. At age 16, I had to compete in the 15 to 18 division (the designated age break in 1963), so I knew I would face tough, older players. The late summer weather was sweltering. I dripped sweat just walking on the court. After a few games in a singles match, I looked like I had just left a swimming pool. After my singles match, where I played well but lost, I got a ride back to my host's house and searched for drinks to restore my lost fluids.

I found a refrigerator in a utility room near the garage door where I came inside the house. When I opened the door, I felt a cold rush, from the frigid air on my body but even more from the shock in my head. I gasped. Every shelf was filled with cans of beer. I had never seen more than one or two such containers together, only when Paul Finney and the older guys in the Lake Junaluska shacks would sneak one inside. In 1963, Methodists in general were strict teetotalers; my parents certainly were. That afternoon I was too surprised and too sheltered to think about taking a can.

Drinking a beer would not be good for my next match either – I was still playing doubles. I gained confidence as I won several matches. I played with abandon, especially with my serve, a particularly important part of a doubles match. Too often, however, on the deuce court, I would go for too much on my second serve and double fault. But I kept my nerve on the ad court and more than once followed a double fault with an ace. Again, double fault and ace. Then finally, an overpowering serve at deuce followed by another ace in the ad court. The semifinals match was on a court in front of the clubhouse. Adults gathered from adjacent courts to see the skinny little kid, sweat pouring down his acned face, hitting unreturnable serves to bigger, stronger, older opponents. But in the next match, the finals, the magic ran out. Still, I was proud to show Mrs. Vest and my parents my second-place trophy, more than a foot tall.

The award has a long louvered piece of metal, with a plate at the bottom that reads: "LA. STATE / JR DBLS 2nd / 1963." At the top, a figure of a young man arches his racket behind his head preparing to serve. His left arm, bent at the elbow, is about to make the toss. This trophy towers above the few smaller local trophies I still have on my bookshelf, marking the summer I played my only regional tennis tournament as a kid.

Last Year in Jackson

In high school, two of my friends and I were all named Bill. We shared not only a name but also much of the school day, including the advanced English and biology periods. The two classes walked across the hallway on the second floor of all-white Murrah High School and swapped subjects in third and fourth periods. Mr. Lyons, our diminutive guru of a science teacher, sometimes led us out the building in his short sleeve shirt and tie, across the drive that swept past the school tennis courts and far wing of the building to a large grassy field, where we collected insects for one of our ongoing projects. In English, Mrs. Crawford would walk us deep into the bowels of the English language, diagramming sentences with increasingly ambiguous independent clauses and difficult choices of subject and object.

We Bills referred to each other by last names: Finger, Sims, and Norton. Sims, who was even skinnier than I, liked to tell tales. "Mr. Jones said he slept in a separate bed from his wife when the heat got too severe." While not an outlandish proposition in this pre-air conditioning era, Sims shuffled such logic aside as he looked down through his big-lensed glasses, lips pursed with anticipation. With a tone of conspiracy, he said, "No wonder they don't have any children." His high-pitched cackle punctuated the punch line, bringing us pre-sexual teenage boys into nervous laughter.

While Sims and I met in high school, among the group of "smart kids" who got placed with the English-biology swap, Norton and I had known each other through church and school on the long march from Dick and Jane to transitive verbs. We weren't playmates in the same neighborhood, no idyllic bike rides in the dusk or rambunctious cub scout meetings in Elbert Bivens' garage. Norton and I knew each other like infantry soldiers might, with a deep South training for the grown-up tasks ahead: segregated schools and churches, regular presence at the largest Methodist church in the state, rigorous devotion to work, dedicated parents who largely avoided talking about race. Norton and Sims helped my days move along. But a sense of true belonging only came when I stepped on a basketball or tennis court. There, I felt the joy of connection with my body, mind, and even my spirit.

Sims and Norton, while not athletes, enjoyed sports. They joined me for the 1964 Canton Invitational Track Meet, to root for the outstanding Murrah High School team. On the 26-mile trip back home to Jackson, time stood still. A cautious but inexperienced driver in my dad's Pontiac, I slowed in the pounding rain on the two-lane asphalt as we approached a sweeping left curve. Maybe I panicked as the wheels lost traction or tried to turn us back into the road too suddenly.

"Hold on," I must have said to the Bills, or thought to myself. The heavy sedan hit the grass and headed toward the bridge embankment on the right, beside a steep drop to the gushing creek. Maybe I prayed, though by age 17 I was skeptical about prayer, even with a Methodist minister for a father. With no seat belts in those days, fate and faith held our safety in the balance.

We came to a stop on a knoll just car lengths before the incline down to the flowing current. We looked at each other, got out of the car, walked around the long side of the unscratched car, saw nothing amiss beyond our throbbing hearts. I took a deep breath, backed the car onto the road, with my buddies directing me, and drove home. I do not remember any of us talking about fear or death or our future that night.

When I finally tiptoed into the house, I woke my dad and told him what happened. His supportive words, glad that all was well, calmed my nerves. Maybe heading down the hall to my bedroom was when I remembered that my grandmother slid off that same highway but with a different ending. I was 11 years old that night when my father knelt at my bed, crying, and told me that Nan was gone. I watched my dad, learning how adults might deal with tragedy, but felt nothing yet of loss.

Leaving Jackson

On the spring afternoons of 1964, I would practice with the Murrah High School tennis team on the courts between the back of the school and the large field filled with insects across the street. Our coach, the school's journalism teacher, mostly threw out some balls and watched us play. When I could, I would go across town to Battlefield Park, the epicenter of tennis in Jackson, to play with Erskine Wells, a Murrah teammate, and others.

That spring, our coach had a dilemma. Erskine and I were close in ability, so he might choose either of us to play singles. The other problem: neither of us had much of a chance to beat Bill Hester. Coach Hunter, the savvy journalism teacher with little coaching experience, put me in boys' doubles and Erskine in mixed doubles. This turned out well for Erskine; he and his partner won handily, all the way to taking the state championship. But our doubles team had to beat two guys on Hester's team at Provine High School. We didn't make it out of the district tournament. My tennis career in Mississippi, as it turned out, was over. I would have no last shot at beating Bill Hester.

During the summer of 1964, while I was at Lake Junaluska, Erskine Wells and other teenagers under Mrs. Vest's guidance played tennis tournaments around Mississippi and neighboring states. I played pick-up matches on concrete courts with any serious player I could find far away in the North Carolina mountains. If someone needed to find me, they looked either at the tiny shacks behind the cafeteria where I worked for a second summer, or at the tennis courts.

"You need to change clothes and get over to the auditorium," the mother of a friend said to me one day, a bit breathless from running up to find me at the courts. I dashed over to the shacks, threw on slacks and my favorite navy alpaca sweater, and hustled down Lakeshore Drive to the site of the quadrennial Southeastern Conference of the Methodist Church.

Every four years, the Methodists elected new bishops to replace those who were retiring. For several days, the ballots had been crowded with multiple candidates in the running for the four spots. Two had been selected, and I knew Dad was in the pack for one of the final two spots. I saw my mother at the back of Stuart Auditorium, which edged against the lapping waters of the beautiful lake. She was gathering up my sister and Dad's parents and sister. My brother and sister were already there. The word went up to the podium that the family was ready.

The photo captured a smiling new bishop-elect on stage with his family. I was used to Dad being at the center of things as president of Millsaps, so this next step did not make me nervous about new limelight for the family. But what it did mean was moving away from Jackson.

We stayed at the Lake through the summer. When the cafeteria finished the season, I said end-of-summer good-byes to my friends, many of them buddies since our family started spending our summers at Lake Junaluska when I was five. My brother shared the driving duties home with Mother, pre-interstate, through the mountains, across Alabama, and finally back into the late-August Mississippi heat.

Dad had returned earlier after his election to wrap up his 12 years as president of Millsaps College. The college had packed our house for the move. I had only a few days to prepare to leave for my new home in Nashville, Tennessee. I re-traced my childhood, driving around Power Elementary, Bailey Junior High, and Murrah High, all in a large adjacent area with a football stadium between them. I walked over to the college tennis courts where I first hit the little round ball. My Junaluska years had led to closer friendships than had my time in Jackson. My anchors in Jackson were my home on the Millsaps campus and my time on tennis and basketball courts. These attachments could travel with me.

We drove north from Jackson, along the Natchez Trace and state highways into central Tennessee. Our furniture and belongings had already arrived in Nashville. My father and mother had immediate responsibilities as the new bishop and bishop's wife, plus making the former bishop's house fit their needs. My brother was off to his junior year of college. My sister was preparing for the eighth grade; I was a rising senior without a friend or tennis court in sight. I felt lost in a big city but also excited for a new adventure. The family had two cars now, so I was able to drive around the metropolitan area to pass the few weeks left of summer, trying to get my bearings geographically if not emotionally. But learning key landmarks and roadways was not enough. I needed help. I could not find a new Erskine Wells or Dorothy Vest to guide me through the Nashville tennis scene. But I did hear about a tournament on the Vanderbilt University hard courts.

The surprise factor helped me grab the biggest win of my young career. Eddie Green was not ready for an unknown in the semi-finals. Then, with confidence and momentum, I slipped through the first set and cruised to the championship.

"Finger Grabs Metro Crown," read the headline in *The Nashville Tennessean* sports section. The story began: "Young Bill Finger, fresh from a Saturday upset of top-seeded Eddie Green, belted Gene Shepherd 7-5, 6-1 yesterday to capture the boys' 18 singles crown in the Nashville Tennis Association's Metropolitan Junior Open."

This signature victory provided more than a single trophy. Transferring a part of myself through time and space, anchored by the familiar rectangular court and bracket format, gave me internal standing for a new life. I still felt disoriented in this new city, certainly, but even when far from a tennis court, I knew that the promise of joy, win or lose, could guide the way.

12

No More Sissy Burgers

Before this trip back to Jackson for the 2019 tournament – 55 years after my win in Nashville – I track down my high school teammates, Erskine Wells and Anne Burwell. During my visit with Carol Ann Vest, both Erskine and Anne call to confirm our meeting later that day at Brent's Drugs. I arrive early at the old drugstore and wait in a booth next to the original soda fountain.

Erskine arrives first. He looks nothing like the 16-year-old in the photo from the Murrah High School newspaper. A thin teenager with a trim haircut and intense, boyish face stands ramrod straight, his Jack Kramer racket angling up at his waist. His left hand holds the state mixed doubles championship trophy; Anne Burwell, his partner, grasps the other side.

I wave from the booth at my old tennis buddy. "Bill!" His buoyant greeting mixes pleasure with disbelief in seeing this white-haired gentleman standing before him more than 50 years since they last swatted forehands in one of Mrs. Vest's signature drills.

"Yeah, we look a lot different don't we!" I would have never recognized this balding, somewhat stocky man as a tennis player except for his light, athletic step, even with what must be an extra 40 pounds from his old playing weight, first at Murrah then on the Ole Miss team.

Anne arrives a few minutes later. I would have recognized her in a crowd of Jacksonians walking down the sidewalk in front of the old Duling School. She has the same tall, straight posture that I remember, confirmed by the state championship photo. Her short, teenage hair flips up on the sides, while today it falls back on either side of her ageless face. She still has the same neat, nothing-fancy-ma'am, thank-you-very-much air about her. Not as angular as her 18-year-old profile, her face has filled out a bit, and she seems more relaxed now than her old photo persona. Even then, though, she looked confident, her racket casually against her leg, no pose.

She gives Erskine a polite hug, one Jacksonian to another – two who stayed here but rarely see each other – and offers her hand to me for a friendly, business-like greeting with a person who left her town so many years ago. We settle in with greetings and coffee.

"Tennis was the most fun I had growing up," Erskine says. An intense, quiet teenager, he has a gregarious style now as he recalls his childhood summers. "One of my parents would drop me off at Battlefield and I would spend the day there, just playing tennis. And remember that little restaurant at the corner where we would get lunch? What was it, the Redwood Motel?"

Anne and I are happy to stroll down this memory lane, smiling as Erskine gestures through his stories. "At that restaurant, there we were, in the little white shorts and shirts we wore in those days. And there were always a bunch of truck drivers and big working-class guys." He smiles, the way a storyteller does, nearing a well-timed punchline. "One day, I ordered a hamburger with just mustard. The waitress said, 'No chili or slaw, nothing else?' 'No, just mustard,' I said. Then she yelled across the room, 'Give me one sissy burger.' The truck drivers all laughed. I felt like sinking to the floor."

We chuckle, remembering this bond of white uniforms and a common purpose, unwavering even among truck drivers.

Our mission was anything but sissy. In the Mississippi heat, a tennis match was taxing, physically and mentally, keeping our minds focused on the next shot, instead of the sweat pouring down our faces.

"Tennis gave me a way to develop friendships," Erskine says. He ticks off the better players in Jackson, Bill Hester, Bill Dockery, and others. "I was shy then, meeting people through tennis was a big help. And, later, tennis helped me in my business life." He got a law degree but did not like practicing law, even though he was welcomed into his father's firm. He switched to financial management. "I developed clients all over the state, many of them coming through tennis friendships. I still think of those days playing at Battlefield and ordering my sissy burgers as some of the happiest times of my life."

After a long pause, Anne asks me why I was playing tennis again and writing about tennis. I pass over several things I could mention before landing on one of the pivotal moments. "One day I was walking my granddaughter along the courts not long after I turned 70, watching my daughter in a group lesson. I heard the sounds off the rackets, you know, thwak, thwak."

"You felt called to play again," Anne says, locking eyes with me across the booth.

"Right. That's exactly it. I realized how much I missed the game... and the competition. Those pops, the balls coming off the strings. Nothing like it. And just like when I turned 35, I thought entering a new category, the 70s, might be fun. Could I do it, still compete, even after decades away from the game?"

Turning to her own story, Anne says, "I was lucky in junior high school. Pat Crockett was a history teacher at Bailey [Junior High] and was the tennis coach, at least for the girls. She got several of us who she thought might be good to practice with her – Susan Gordon, Lynn Biggs, some others. We would practice at Bailey, and she would take us over to the

Riverside Drive courts to practice as well."

When Anne went from junior high to the much larger Murrah High School in the tenth grade, she felt a bit overwhelmed. "I don't have fond memories of high school," Anne continues. "Murrah had so many people, packed halls between classes. I needed something that I was good at, among a smaller group of people. Tennis gave me the niche I needed."

The conversation turns casual. Neither Erskine nor Anne offers more about tennis, and I suddenly am not sure how to proceed. Should I probe about their life in Jackson today or look for more common tennis history to explore?

I decide to share my impressions of Jackson after my long absence. "As I left the interstate coming in from the airport, the potholes were the first thing I noticed. I am so surprised about how run down the city looks."

They both nod. "Yes, Jackson has changed a lot," Erskine says.

"I'm planning to go to the Civil Rights Museum tomorrow," I say.

"It's excellent, just excellent," Anne says with the same serious, caring face she had when speaking about herself as a high schooler needing a niche. Erskine offers no comment.

"When I went to Randolph Macon College [in Virginia]," Anne continues, "my freshman year a professor asked me what I thought of the poll tax in Mississippi. I had never even heard of the poll tax. We never talked about race issues in our family or in school."

Anne returned to Jackson where she taught at St. Andrew Episcopal School, founded in 1947, well before the white flight schools opened as desegregation came. She worked there until retiring this summer. The school, Anne says, has always focused on academic excellence, diversity, and commitment to the world around us. Now she works, at age 72, as a reading tutor and dyslexia therapist. She hasn't played tennis for more than 20 years and never played serious tournaments beyond her 20s.

Erskine continued to play serious tennis, including regional tournaments, into his 50s. Injuries have ended his competitive career for now, but he thinks he may try to get back in shape and go at it again.

I tell Anne and Erskine about the tournament at River Hills and my match times in singles and doubles. "Maybe you can come out and watch one of them. I play Bill Hester in doubles." Anne explains she has commitments with grand-children and work, but Erskine thinks he will be able to come out.

As the conversation winds down, the nagging feeling that I have not been able to pinpoint during my two days in Jackson becomes a bit clearer. I feel some "otherness" – not because of the color of my skin, the defining issue for this town, but because of my dual citizenship, as it were. I was once a Mississippian, with deep roots on both sides of my family, but when I left as a rising high school senior, I never really looked back. I knew this place for my first 17 years, that formative time, raised by parents who grew up in two small Mississippi towns – certainly, I have standing here. But a revolution has come and gone, leaving a wake of new opportunity competing with deeply ingrained white supremacy. Does my dormant citizenship give me standing in making judgments about progress in Mississippi?

As a kid, I joined in the familiar singsong, "Save your Dixie cups 'cause the South will rise again." If the Confederacy has not risen in structure, its flag and monuments are certainly in the national news. National Football League players kneel at the national anthem, echoing the black power fists from the U.S. Olympic sprinters in 1968. I lived through that Olympic moment and watched Colin Kaepernick take a knee in response to the spate of police killings of inner-city black people.

How all of this affects my Mississippi identity today in Jackson, talking with my old high school teammates, I don't know. But I do not feel comfortable discussing the shortcomings of this city with Erskine and Anne and asking why they decided to make their homes and raise their families here.

Tennis Partner Arrives

Erskine, Anne, and I take a few photos and head our separate ways. As much as I enjoy this visit, and my time with Carol Ann Vest, I feel more relaxed as I pull into the River Hills Tennis Club. I am headed for a practice round with my friend John Walton, the top ranked 70-and-over player in North Carolina. A quiet, salt-of-the-earth man who grew up on a farm, he has built his life around tennis, directing tennis programs and a college team an hour west of my home in Raleigh.

When I walk onto the court, I unwind my body around my forehand and slice backhand. Running down some of John's sharp-angled shots generates sweat and effort, satisfaction with good shots and patience with the not-so-good. My main challenge returning to serious tennis after so many years is consistency. I have good shots at times, but some very bad misses as well.

After an extended warm-up, cross-court rallies with forehands and backhands as well as some down-the-line hitting, John wants to play a set. Good idea, keep sharp on shot selection in game and set situations. I tire quickly in the humid afternoon heat, totally soaked in sweat. I realize that long rallies and running for drop shots could tire me quickly in this heat.

Odd, I thought, resting after 20 minutes of hard hitting and a 25-minute set. I have only known John about a year – only seen him four or five times ever – but feel more relaxed with him this afternoon than I did with Erskine and Anne two hours earlier. Of course, I have not seen them for more than 50 years, so it's logical that I would feel more familiar with a friend from Raleigh. As Erskine, Anne, and I swapped stories of going from little Power and Duling elementary schools to big Bailey Junior High, and finally to mighty Murrah High School, we shared pictures in our minds of that era. We weren't always in each other's videos of the mind, but some of the time we were, on the hard courts by Murrah or across town on the green clay courts under the direction of Mrs. Vest.

What I had in common with my new friend, John Walton, and my very old friends from Murrah High School, was the game of tennis, and conversations that it spawned, from tournament seedings and opponents to cafes and sissy burgers.

Museum, Galloway, Battlefield

The next day, Thursday, I am free before my first-round match, scheduled for 3:30. I want to learn more about Jackson and how my memories affect my feelings now. My first stop is the two-year-old Mississippi Civil Rights Museum, which opened with its companion museum, side-by-side, the Mississippi History Museum. They share an entrance and a broad lawn on a downtown street near the State Capitol and the old fairgrounds, used as a makeshift jail for civil rights protesters in the 1960s.

In my seventh grade Mississippi history class, I competed with my all-white classmates to compile the thickest scrapbook with brochures on such notables as Natchez antebellum homes and Picayune cucumbers. Nothing about Medgar Evers working for the NAACP ever came up. That year, age 13, I was part of the 64 percent white majority in Jackson. As I walk into the museum in 2019, Jackson is 17 percent White and 82 percent African American.

The Mississippi Civil Rights Museum has seven sections laid out like slices of a pizza.

In an early section, I read the list of men (mostly) who

were lynched, and look at photos and reconstructions of those tragedies. I feel sad and weary from all the pain and hate that lived in Mississippi.

In the segment covering the Jim Crow era, if I step into an area where African Americans were not meant to walk, such as sidewalks, museum sensors trigger a voice telling me to move off and to the side. As instructed, I step aside to a space identified as "safe" for a black person. Even on a museum visit, I feel angry, surprised that I am uncomfortable, not allowed to stroll through the museum however I want, without a voice telling me to move off my path. The design transports a white man into a tiny piece of a black man's world.

I need some restoration and head to the center of the museum, called "This Little Light of Mine." In this large room, where the seven museum sections meet, a sculpture filled with light and sound gets louder as sensors in the floor respond to more people. As the sculpture pulsates and changes colors while the familiar song grows louder, I feel lighter, with new energy for the next gallery.

Standing beside photos of the Freedom Riders, a black man about my age is talking to a group of African American visitors. "I just happened to be on the sidewalk beside the bus station," he says. "My mother had told me to stay away from there. But when the police came to arrest the Freedom Riders, they swept me up with them." He and I were contemporaries in Jackson. Now, standing just a few feet apart, I wonder how growing up in this segregated city affected us as adults.

The information on Methodist ministers, and especially Dr. W.B. Selah, stops me in my tracks. From about age seven until age 17, every Sunday morning from September through May, I sat in the Galloway Methodist Church balcony listening to Dr. Selah preach.

In June 1963, just before I boarded the bus for Lake Junaluska, Dr. Selah stunned the all-white congregation he had served for 18 years. African American students had walked up the imposing steps at the front of the Galloway sanctuary, just a block from the State Capitol. When they requested a seat for the worship service, the ushers turned them away; only Whites could enter this house of God, the most prominent Methodist church in the state. Dr. Selah learned during the service what had happened; he cut his sermon short and announced that he was resigning as pastor.

"Selah's action divided the community," the label below Dr. Selah's photo reads in the museum. "Some opposed 'politics' in the church, while others praised his principled stand."

The museum presents historical periods with depth and pathos, while also providing a place of recovery and rejuvenation from a painful journey through time. The sculpture, "This Little Light of Mine," is visible outside at night through large windows, a symbol of hope for a better day.

On my next stop, just a few blocks from the museum, I park at the side entrance of Galloway Church, which Dr. Selah led from 1945 to 1963. I ring the bell for admission and soon find myself in the hall at the door to Dr. Selah's old study, chatting with the church administrator. After I say who I am, that my father was president of Millsaps College, she kindly agrees to show me the church.

"This is where I met with Dr. Selah regularly on Saturday mornings," I tell her. "It was part of my work on the God and Country award in Boy Scouts." She leads me down the familiar corridor past other offices. "Has the church remained as big, as prominent as it was when I was here?"

"I don't think we ever really recovered from Dr. Selah's departure," she says.

As we move toward the sanctuary, I glance up the stairs to the right towards a lounge area where my youth group sometimes met. An image from one Sunday night flashes into focus. "We have received a request from a Methodist youth group in the north," the adult leader said. He read the letter, where the youth asked us why we have such a hard time getting along with Negroes and why we keep them separate.

Our group sat in silence for a long time until finally, one young woman, a senior, said, "There are just so many of them."

Discomfort stirred in my belly. Perhaps in that moment of 1962 my unconscious was trying to process the dichotomy of "them and us," a tenet inconsistent with the faith that anchored this massive building. But I lacked the tools at age 16 to sort through such feelings, much less manage a comment.

My mind goes back to the 2019 visit at hand, as my guide motions me to our left. I move through the side door into the sanctuary. The pews in the large semicircular layout look worn, like an old house needing a facelift. Small pillars throughout support the balcony, where I sat with my mother and siblings Sunday after Sunday, listening to Dr. Selah preach. I can almost see Dr. Selah behind the pulpit, short in stature, serious in faith, principled in action. I realize now that while I don't remember his sermons, I did feel safe in the world of faith he conveyed. His quiet way echoed the kindness of my father.

Battlefield

Before returning for a pre-match rest at the Airbnb, I have one more stop: Battlefield Park. No more sissy burgers were served at the dilapidated store on the corner. Houses on adjacent streets lie tired, in disrepair. Tall, stately trees have disappeared, along with the energy of park visitors and the sound of tennis games. Near the corner of the park is a brick wall with a clean green sign, "Battlefield Tennis Center." Hours and fee schedules are listed, with a smaller sign below it, "Dorothy Vest Tennis Center Pro Shop."

The rubico courts appear to have been abandoned for many years, with sagging nets on a few but no playable surfaces left. The fence around the courts is locked, so I walk out onto the hard courts that run behind the rubico row, once so beautiful and pristine before an opening tournament match. Clearly, no one is paying a fee to play here.

"Can I help you?" I turn back toward the clubhouse and see an African American woman at the gate to the hard courts. Heavy, wearing a dress, she does not look like a tennis player.

"I used to play tennis here when Dorothy Vest ran things," I say.

"Really, wow," she says. "Come in and see the clubhouse. We're trying to get things going again." I walk inside with her and meet a second woman. The walls are bare, with no tennis equipment in sight.

"We're trying to get some teams playing on the hard courts," one of the women says. "Looks like we'll have two or three teams for the first league. We're going to have a re-opening of the clubhouse in the next month or so."

I explain that I am visiting Jackson and have recently met with Carol Ann, Dorothy Vest's oldest child. "I'll tell her about your re-opening plans."

Neither of the women are tennis players, but they seem to have good energy for getting a league going. Without a charismatic leader like Dorothy Vest, not to mention much-needed funding from a money-strapped Jackson budget, success faces long odds. But who knows? Maybe a bit of tennis will once again find its way onto the Vest Tennis Center.

13

Southern Championships

The luck of the tournament draw does not provide a shot at redemption against Bill Hester. Instead of Hester, I am matched against the No. 1 seed, Padj Bolton. Thursday afternoon, May 2, 2019, I take the court. I win the coin toss and choose to receive.

Bolton double faults twice, and I keep the ball in play on the other points. First game for the underdog. At 2-2, Bolton hits his 6-feet, 2-inch stride. His forehand begins to overpower me; I hit late, weak backhands, setting up his winners. His serve picks up pace, winning him more and more "free points" – either outright or on the "serve plus one" second shot. No umpire is calling this first round match in Jackson. The USTA did rank this as a Category II tournament, one level below the four national championships held for seniors in 2019.

Bolton and I play on the green clay, the middle of the three courts at the far end of the club, away from the upscale clubhouse. Only a few onlookers are in the bleachers between banks of courts. I nod at my old friend, Erskine Wells, who has made time from his financial management business to come out.

Behind 1-0 in the second set, I realize that Bolton's forehand and serve are hurting me the most. I start to hit to his backhand whenever possible. I hold serve, picking on his backhand. Then, on his serve, I back up two feet behind the baseline and get better returns in play. He holds, but with a struggle. I win my service game again, leveling the second set at 2-2. But he adjusts too. Too often, I hit a decent forehand up the line to his backhand, but he sees it coming and runs around it to blast an inside-out forehand. I have too much court to cover to reach my backhand corner. I have several ads to pick up more games but go down to the top seed, 6-2, 6-2. My lessons for the day are to get better against players at his level: adjust earlier, stay confident, and vary my shot selection.

Walking off the court, I pause and exchange greetings with Erskine. Then he turns to my opponent. "Hi Padj, I'm Erskine Wells. We've played in tournaments a few years back." Padj smiles and they chat a little. Then Erskine looks back my way. "Wow, I was really impressed at how hard you guys hit it. You had some great driving backhands Bill. I can tell I'll have to work at my game to get back to that level." I smile, proud of how I played and glad that Erskine saw the match.

After a shower, I watch my friend from Raleigh, Carlos Garcia, play his first round in the 55-and-over event. Carlos has dark wavy hair, with streaks of gray, covered by his tightly worn hat. A gregarious teaching pro at the Raleigh Racquet Club, and former college coach at the University of Tennessee, Chattanooga, Carlos has spent his life with tennis. He has won national championships in doubles.

I pull a chair under a bit of shade near the back corner of the courts where I played earlier. Even at 5 o'clock the Mississippi sun is brutal, with temperatures in the 90s. My tall, lanky friend has a long stride, familiar to me from the few lessons I've had with him in Raleigh. I watch his footwork, using quick steps to get in position so that his swing is at the best level possible. His shot preparation proves decisive, finally breaking a tough opponent's spirit in the long fifth game to take the lead at 3-2. Carlos maintains his intensity, moving to a comfortable win, 6-2, 6-2.

The next morning, on Friday, 70-and-over matches start

the day. The winners from yesterday play the quarterfinals. In my part of the bracket, Bolton beats Hester decisively, giving up only one game. The two first-round losers in our section of the draw meet in the consolation bracket. I play Steve Duffel, who lost to Hester in the first round and now loses to me by the same score. For a head-to-head match-up with Hester, for now, I can only base my comparison on winning three more games against Bolton than Hester did.

Doubles – Another Shot

First round of doubles, Finger and Walton against Hester and Burris. A big lefty from Texas, Burris plays the deuce court, putting a wall of forehand volleys against any shots we aim down the middle. Hester has some extra weight to carry but has less court to cover in doubles than singles and still has his lifelong shot-making ability.

In the first set, Burris is a beast, picking off my returns of Hester's tough serves while also hitting great angles on his serve returns. Hester hits clean, solid shots. Walton and I have never played doubles together, but we have a stoic determination. I get my serve in and return well; he does the same. But one break of my serve is enough to go down a set, 6-4.

The second set starts just as close, each point important. One game I double fault the first two points, but keep my composure and rally to hold. As the set moves closer to the finish line, I move to the baseline to serve again. At 15-love, serving to Hester in the ad court, I put my toss a bit more to my left, about "11 o'clock" instead of "12." I snap my wrist at the height of my reach and hit a wicked kick serve deep in the backhand corner. Hester barely reaches for it as it whizzes by. Later in the game, another ace in the same corner. I hold serve. We level the set at six games each.

Walton serves first in the seven-point tiebreak and double

faults. But we get one of their two service points, now down only 1-2. My turn to serve two points. We get the first point to tie it at 2-2, but then I also double fault. Again, down a mini break as they serve at 3-2. Hester gets one of his two service points, but that is their last. We take the tiebreak, 7-4. One set each. We all sit and rest, drinking water.

We get an early break in the third set and take a 4-2 lead. Hester then steps up to serve. Walton and I hit solid returns, but Burris reaches his long arm out into the middle of the court to hit winning volleys. Hester reaches their first ad point. I bounce at the baseline, ready for a serve to my backhand. When it comes, I move forward, turn my hips, and plant my right foot to slice a low return. At the last second, I sense Burris is moving to mid-court to cut off my return. I adjust. Clean winner down his alley. Deuce.

Hester holds again on the deuce court against Walton. Their second ad point. This time, as Hester's toss goes up, I take a step to my left and hit a forehand drive toward Hester's backhand. I sail it past Burris' outstretched left hand. It lands deep in the alley outside of Hester's reach. Deuce.

Again, despite a good return from Walton, our opponents work themselves into a third straight ad point. As Hester serves, I step left this time and get the forehand swing I want. My sharp, low dipping shot past Burris falls right at Hester's feet. Deuce.

This time, Walton hits a winner on his return, and we have our first ad. I get ready for another winning forehand but dump an easy serve into the net. Walton has said very little the entire match, but this time offers a boost: "Give him a chance to hit it." I can feel his energy rising, and he gets us still another ad with a great return. This time, I hit a sharp forehand at Bill's feet. Our game. I serve at 5-2, get my serves in, and Walton pounces on every return at the net. Our match: 4-6, 7-6, 6-2.

"Your serve was the difference," Hester says as we walk

toward the clubhouse, where a growing number of spectators have been watching the match since the second-set tiebreak. "I was returning well and then you got those aces on me. I think we would've had it without those aces."

In the plush locker room at the main club house, the hot shower washes off the sweat. My mind wanders as I let the victory soak in: Does beating my childhood nemesis, even in doubles, mean I step onto a new plateau as a tennis player? Don't childhood patterns affect adult thinking? Or do I need to beat someone like Bolton? Maybe I just need to get better and not worry about winning. Isn't that the main lesson, to control what I can, my own shots, win or lose? As I leave the club that evening, I smile, content with a very good win.

• 14 •

Gratitude and Freedom

Saturday morning, a downpour sounds a sharp staccato on the River Hills patio. A few players call in to be sure their matches are postponed and stay away, going out to breakfast with wives or doubles partners. Others with a scheduled morning match show up despite the rain, our home away from home. The heavy clouds foretell the day ahead in Jackson, much like the dark days of Mississippi's past prepared me for my visit to the Civil Rights Museum. But the storm before me only affects tennis games. No lives lost. No mistrials of justice. No restrictions on where I can walk.

Most traveled to Jackson only to play tennis, not to revisit the state's past. On this pilgrimage to my hometown, I too am focusing now on the details of swinging a racket. Winning the doubles match on Friday fed my hunger. I want more, to win another match, now into the doubles semifinals. And, after winning one round in the consolation singles on Friday, I look forward to my next match against a veteran of these 70-and-over tournaments.

Tournament director Dave Randall sits with us on the patio, looking at his weather app from time to time. "Looks like there might be a window between segments of the storm in the afternoon," he says, lifting his eyes from the phone to the dozen or so players lounging about. "We might be able to get some matches in around two if the rain holds off for a couple of hours to let the courts dry enough to play."

Several ask about playing on the four indoor courts in the large tennis facility at the far end of the Har-Tru courts. "Members have scheduled matches on those courts," Randall says. "They knew the tournament would be going on. We don't have any access to those courts."

Settling onto the patio for a while, I shift my thoughts from Jackson and tennis strategy to the players around me, none of whom I have met before the tournament. In one conversation, two musicians share stories of retiring from major orchestras, selling instruments, and moving into more serious tournament tennis. In a flat midwestern accent, the one African American player I remember seeing on the courts the day before is telling stories about life in Chicago. I wonder if he managed to learn the game in an integrated public park program.

Building friendships with tennis players from across the country will take time, years – seeing them at future tournaments, finding common interests beyond tennis, recounting tennis experiences and ideas from fellow travelers. As I ponder issues of friendship in later life and the role of tennis players as my new tribe, I hear the tournament director.

"There will be no matches before 2 p.m.," he says. "Even if the rain stops, it will take that long for the courts to dry enough to play." I decide to make one more stop in Jackson.

Exiting the club, I reach Interstate 55 in about five minutes, and in another 10 minutes, I park beside a popular bakery. The airy two-story lobby in the building has a balcony and large plants, which invites me upstairs into a large independent bookstore.

"Hi, can I help you?" The friendly staff person greets me as I pass by piles of bestsellers beside the information desk. I spot thick copies of the Mueller report, which has just been released.

"Yes. I wonder if I could leave my book for your shelves,"

I say. "It's a memoir on midlife issues. I published it about three years ago. It has a chapter on Jackson, including material about my father, who was president of Millsaps College."

The person looks at me more closely as she takes the book and reads my name on the cover. "I know you. I'm Pat Twente, my maiden name. We went to Murrah together."

"Of course," I say. An image of a teenage Pat Twente on a tennis court somehow curls up from some long-buried brain cell. "Didn't you play on the tennis team, maybe in junior high or high school?"

"Yes, I did play tennis in school," she says, walking toward the administrative offices to the right of the information desk. She hands my book to the person behind a computer, explaining what I want.

"I'm in town for a seniors tennis tournament at River Hills," I say. "I'm also writing about the role of tennis in my life, as I get back into playing tournaments."

I browse through the excellent, well-stocked store. I can see why southern writers have been launching books in this store for decades. Maybe I will read from my new tennis book here one day. Before I leave, Pat tells me they will put my first book on their shelves.

Another Shot

I drive back to my Airbnb, take a nap, get lunch, and head back to the club, even though play looks doubtful. When I check in with the tournament director, he gives me surprising news. "Turns out that several of the indoor courts are available. Your opponent would like to play. He should be available later this afternoon, around 5 o'clock. Since it's indoor and not on clay, it's your choice. You don't have to play."

"I'd like to play. It's what I came here for after all."

I find John Curtin already waiting on our indoor court.

He beat his first-round opponent 6-0, 6-0, then lost to the second seeded player in two competitive sets. I watched part of his loss the day before and knew he would be a tough but beatable opponent. His unusual serving motion, a kind of windup like a baseball pitcher, does not produce much pace. Nor does he seem fast covering the court, oddly wearing long baggy white pants and a white jacket even in the heat. His racket covers are frayed on all the edges, looking decades old, and he wears a kind of skull cap.

In the first set, I try to attack his soft serve, sometimes hitting winners but too often letting the slow pace throw off my rhythm, dumping the ball in the net. I follow my serve and my returns of his serve to the net as much as I can, hitting what I think are winning volleys. Again and again, Curtin lunges and stabs the volleys back. Still, I take the lead in the first set, hitting winning shots off his returns. But then I start making too many errors, and the set slips away. He keeps at this dogged style: getting balls back in play, rarely hitting winners, and taking advantage of my errors. He wins the second set more easily. Curtin over Finger, 6-4, 6-3.

In the locker room at the end of the hall, past other indoor courts, I pull off my soaked shirt and shorts and sag onto the hard bench. Frustrated with my errors, regretting that I didn't make a stronger commitment to my attacking shots, I am settling into the agony of defeat. Then I notice another player around the corner, half-dressed and nursing his foot.

"Hi. I think we practiced together the other day, right? You're the guy from California, into the 60s for the first year."

"Right, Matt Houseman."

"I'm Bill Finger, in the 70s. Just lost a consolation round. We played indoors. How did you do?"

"Unfortunately, I got beat rather handily. And I've hurt my foot. Was just testing it a little."

"So sorry about your foot. I thought you'd do well the way you were hitting with me the other day."

"Well, the injury slowed me down. And he was a good player."

The conversation brings me back to a more even keel, my preoccupation with losing is fading. I feel even better after a shower. I will learn something from my defeat, especially how to concentrate on limiting unforced errors. I have no injury. And, I do not have a dilemma like Houseman: go to the Atlanta tournament with an injury or fly back to California.

Oddly, I start feeling grateful, even happy. I played well in many ways against a player at about my level and held my own in a close loss. Facing three different types of players in the singles draw has been fun and instructive. I'm gradually discovering how my game stacks up with others in regional and national tournaments.

At the tournament dinner that night, I sit with my doubles partner, John Walton. Photos from the tournament cycle through a loop on a screen at the front, including one of Walton and me in doubles. Three guys at the table are discussing seedings at the Atlanta tournament next week. They do not welcome us into this or any other conversation. John eats quickly and moves on to greet a few old friends. I suddenly feel a bit alone in my old city. Then I see Carlos, the pro from Raleigh, now the favorite to win the 55 division on Sunday. I move over to his table, feeling at home immediately with Carlos and his friends from past tournaments.

As the tournament dinner winds down, I linger, chatting with a few new acquaintances from hanging out on the patio during the rain. A phone call from my doubles partner, now back at his motel, surprises me. He talks about the draws for the next day. Because of the rain today, the semifinals will be Sunday morning, and the finals in the afternoon. John is in the semis in singles and doubles, and he has an early afternoon flight home.

"Bill, I just don't see how we'll have time to play the doubles finals if we win in the semis," he says. "I'm afraid that if we win, we will have to default in the finals." During dinner, we talked briefly about this possibility, so I am not totally surprised by his reasoning. "I think the fair thing to do is to go ahead and default in the semis tonight. Can you tell Dave so he can plan the schedule for tomorrow?"

As John finishes, I glance across the room and see Dave, the tournament director. I am not sure that we need to default tonight, in terms of tournament protocol, but John has played in so many senior tournaments, and this is one of my first. He is always gracious to players and officials, so I defer. "Sure, I'll let him know we'll default."

Not ready to return to an Airbnb with no working television, I linger in the bar area, which is packed and still buzzing about the controversial finish of the Kentucky Derby. Finally, those guests filter out. I stay at the bar watching the Golden State Warriors and the Houston Rockets in the NBA playoffs.

Two African American women servers and I are the only people left. As I nurse my beer, I feel disappointed in not being able to advance in the doubles tomorrow. But I also am aware of how grateful I am to be here in Jackson at all. I have enough money to fly into town, rent a room, pay the entrance fee, and rent a car. My body is healthy enough to run miles chasing a little ball around a court. I wonder what fate the two women closing the bar now will have in their 70s.

Sunday Doubles – What Might Have Been

The matches started early Sunday. By the time I check out of my Airbnb and reach the club, Walton's semifinal singles match is nearly over. The day before, he beat the number 3 seed and today faces Norm Chryst, the number 2 seed. Walton has beaten Chryst over the years, but not today. He loses quickly, 6-1, 6-3, so he is finished with his singles well before mid-morning. Then, I learn that the other semifinals doubles played the night before on the indoor courts. No one told us. With Walton's quick defeat in singles, we would probably have had time to play our semifinals doubles match mid-morning, with enough time to play the finals before his flight.

Why did we default so soon? Did I let John talk me into something I didn't really want to do on the phone the night before? The conversation bounces around in my head as I sit in street clothes watching others play. *Why didn't the director tell us to hold off until Sunday morning if he knew some matches were being played indoors? Was I right to defer to John's sportsmanship and experience at these tournaments?*

The thoughts scroll through and out of my brain as I enjoy seeing some of the legends of senior tennis in the United States. Lester Sack in the 80s and King Van Nostrand in the 85s are among the top ranked players in the world in their age divisions. Both win their divisions easily. Then, I watch Carlos win his finals in the 55s, happy for him as he shows me his cool glass trophy. I am getting acquainted with major tournament tennis, including the uncertainties of match times, weather, partners, and airplane schedules.

While the tournament is winding down around 1 p.m., the River Hills Club is packed with a Sunday brunch crowd. I splurge on the $25 smorgasbord, complete with whatever you can eat, from a shrimp bowl and a carving table to a luscious dessert table.

Inside the bar area, a few African Americans are scattered among the white guests. "You look very familiar. Don't I know you?" a middle-aged white woman asks an African American man.

After several questions about possible mutual acquaintances, the man says, "Maybe at the Medical School. I was doing a residency here."

"Of course. Now I remember," she says. They review past times and friends, not a trace of awkwardness or hesitancy about the role of race, then or today in Jackson. I wonder what the white families in earshot of the conversation or the black servers clearing the tables might be thinking. I wonder how different Mississippi is today, so many years after I left, and how many black doctors work at the University of Mississippi Medical Center.

Restless now, tired of watching men I don't know in the few remaining matches, I go to the airport. I almost make an earlier flight to Atlanta but instead find a quiet gate area to wait for my scheduled flight. An hour into rambling thoughts, Carlos shows up, trophy safely tucked into his carry-on bag, and starts telling me tennis stories.

"Yes, we were the Tennis Family of the Year," he says of the award the U.S. Tennis Association bestows, describing how his parents encouraged all their kids to play. Carlos made tennis his career. I now have brushed shoulders with two of the USTA families of the year – the Vests and the Garcias. And I've mingled with the Hester family, an icon in USTA lore, thanks to Slew Hester's role in launching the US Open tennis site in Flushing Meadow, NY.

Carlos adds to these notable associations a story about the Davis Cup, the global team competition held annually. For the 2000 Davis Cup matches, the United States players could bring their personal coaches. Carlos was the coach at the time for one of the Davis Cup team members and traveled with him to Spain.

After a night match, where fans were rowdy in the European style of Davis Cup competition, the USA team went out for dinner. Standing in the old town square, busy in the Spanish style of late-night dining, people recognized John McEnroe, the captain of the Davis Cup team that year, and picked up the heckling style from the match.

"At first, it was just a few jeers and gestures," Carlos says as we sit waiting for our plane. "Then, it heated up. Soon, people started throwing things. We all circled around McEnroe and formed a human shield. Then, we walked in a kind of circle back to our hotel. We all got back safely. No harm done."

Carlos flashes his big toothy smile, long wavy hair bouncing as he holds out his arms in a pantomime version of that late-night rescue of the Davis Cup captain. He laughs more as he tells story after story of his long tennis career as player and coach.

Devil's Sanctuary

Several weeks after returning to Raleigh, I receive *Devil's Sanctuary: An Eyewitness History of Mississippi Hate Crimes*, mailed by a cousin I saw in Jackson. The book recounts the murders of Medgar Evers and so many more, some famous and others not. The two authors, a lawyer and a journalist, both grew up and worked in Mississippi and add their own insights to the histories. The lawyer, Alex Alston, was a student at Millsaps College when my dad was president.

"Millsaps College kept its integrity throughout these turbulent times," Alston wrote in *Devil's Sanctuary*, "through strong and fearless faculty led by a courageous, moderate Mississippi native and Methodist minister, President Homer Ellis Finger Jr., who forever will be remembered as protecting the sanctity of academic freedom."

For many years, I have pondered whether my father fell into the category of liberal Southerners who Martin Luther King Jr. took to task in his *Letter from a Birmingham Jail*. Alston, the Millsaps graduate and eyewitness author, helps me see my father another way. Dad grew up in a little town in Mississippi, where *his* father ran a farm supply store, helping small farmers, Black and White, survive the Depression. While my dad was trained at Yale Divinity School, he was cut as much from his father's cloth as from a clerical collar. Dad's tenure as a college president during the Civil Rights era challenged him to maintain the integrity of Millsaps College, his "store." His job was to protect academic freedom from the threats of the

Mississippi State Sovereignty Commission.

One of Alston's stories brings an unexpected smile as I remember my week in Jackson. In the chapter called "Mississippi's Legal Jungle," Alston describes a dilemma he had in 1971 as president of the Jackson Junior Bar Association. Alston invited two young black lawyers in town to participate. But he could not find a place that would allow the Junior Bar Association to hold an integrated meeting. Finally, he called the manager of a facility he knew with a large dining space and explained that this would bring substantial sums if they held their regular meetings there. The manager of the seven-year-old club agreed.

Alex Alston led the first inter-racial meeting of lawyers in Jackson at the dining room of the River Hills Tennis Club.

If my father protected the sanctity of academic freedom during the Civil Rights era, tennis provided me with a place of sanctity for my psyche. The predictable parameters of a tennis court, along with the engaging, in-the-moment allure of competition, provided solace, a home base for a sensitive young white boy. Tennis nurtured me like a church. I am grateful for people like Dorothy Vest, who encouraged me to play tennis. In old age, I have a new tennis season, with new ways to understand the world in which I live and play and worship.

Part III

Bill Finger (left) and Tom Farquhar, doubles partner at
Duke University, 1968

● 15 ●

Duke University, Finding My Base

In the spring of 2019, at my 50th reunion at Duke University, I make my way through the sprawling athletic complex. Walking past several new buildings, including an indoor tennis facility, I find the reception for returning athletes. Only a handful of people are here. Most are standing around the hors d'oeuvres table, sampling large shrimp, small roast beef sandwiches, and an assortment of salads and sweets. After filling a plate, I greet another former Duke competitor.

"I played soccer in the fall and baseball in the spring," he says, as we share cocktail talk on our respective Duke sports histories. "In those days, I could play both sports. There were no year-round practices. It was fun, even though hardly anyone came to see us play."

"Tennis was the same way," I say. "We only had a spring season, unlike college teams now. I played pickup basketball in the fall, through the first semester." We look at each other's gray hair and smile, both of us still lean and athletic. Despite 50 years gone, we bond, sharing our common ground in the "minor sports" with no scholarships and few perks.

"I loved the game and the competition," I add. "Practices every day with teammates. All that time together on the courts and some traveling around the conference. I made some life-long friendships. And it saw me through some rough patches." As the baseball player and I swap stories, I see Alice Weldon come into the large reception area, and I excuse myself.

Alice is a lifelong friend, as is another former Duke ath-lete, Mike Jordan, whom I may see today as well. They grew up in various North Carolina towns while I lived in Jackson, Mississippi. But we spent every summer together on a quaint little street at the Southeastern Methodist Assembly at Lake Junaluska, NC, a picturesque area nestled among the Appalachian Mountains. Our fathers, all Methodist minis-ters, owned cottages there. The three of us deepened connec-tions year after year, through swimming lessons and hide and seek games to campfire songs and youth group gatherings, and finally into college choices. Duke University, then with reduced tuition for Methodist ministers' children in North Carolina, was the de facto choice for Alice and Mike.

Alice played on the women's basketball club team, finish-ing her college years before Duke had a formal intercollegiate team. Women's athletics expanded at Duke after the 1972 Title IX amendments to federal education law. Mike was a wrestler, another minor sport, and conference champion in his weight class our senior year.

After Alice and I greet each other, she asks about my ten-nis buddies. "There were two guys who roomed together, right? Are they coming?"

"Right, Tom Farquhar and Don Berns. They roomed together their last three years and remained close friends all through the years. Sadly, Don died a few years ago. He had Parkinson's disease." I pause, letting the news, spoken aloud, soak into the open space. I suddenly miss them both.

"Tom sometimes comes to reunions but couldn't this time. He's expecting a new grandchild." We talk a little more. She has other close friends from her Duke days and has plans with them for the weekend.

"I'm off to the Bryan Center now," I tell her as I prepare to leave for the large student union building next to the famous Duke Chapel. "I think I told you. The Alumni office has arranged a display of books that people from the 50th reunion class have written. My book is there, so I'm going to see the display."

"I'll try to stop by and see it. You know I love your book."

"Thanks Alice. Tell Mike I'm sorry I'll miss him. I'll see him at Junaluska soon."

Walking back toward the main campus, I reach the large new tennis stadium with multi-tiered rows of seats and a scoreboard large enough to highlight more than a dozen Atlantic Coast Conference (ACC) Championships won by the men's and women's tennis teams.

In the 1960s, a small set of wooden bleachers in this very spot could easily accommodate the handful of fans who watched our team hit flat strokes on slow, green clay composition courts. There was no women's team then. With the new stadium came a shift from the clay to the hard, asphalt-like coating used throughout college tennis programs and at the U.S. Open tennis championships.

Some familiar landmarks still look the same. Behind me, at the end of the parking lot, stands the old gym where I dressed for tennis practice for four years. In the mid-1960s, before tennis scholarships came to Duke and most colleges, we had only a spring season. During the fall and winter, I played pickup basketball games in the gym above our dingy locker room and when available, in the varsity basketball arena next door, made famous later by Mike Krzyzewski and his national championship teams.

Basketball and Roberta Flack

In the fall of 1964, when I learned that Duke had a fall deadline for early admission, I crafted my application essay well before the final date. On a visit to Duke with my father, we saw the Chapel, the main academic buildings, and the student union. I never thought about looking for tennis courts or talking to the tennis coach. The biggest decision before college was about living arrangements, not about sports. A letter from Duke arrived in the summer of 1965 asking about any roommate preferences. Among other questions: Would I be willing to room with a Negro?

My father must have been away the day I opened the letter and showed it to my mother.

"Oh, I don't think you want to live with a Negro," she said, adding something like: "You'll have enough to think about your first semester without that added issue."

As I sat in my room that day, the heaviness of race and integration crept into my head. *Maybe she is right. College will be challenging enough without dealing with the race issue.* My reflections never got beyond the "added issue." I did not think about a person, about sharing daily routines with a Negro, how that might affect him as well as me. The only Negro peer I had ever known was our maid's daughter, Jeannette, when we tossed a baseball back and forth. But those visits stopped when we were about 10. I checked the box: I preferred *not* to have a Negro roommate.

Tom Farquhar must have also received a letter from Duke asking whether he would be willing to room with an African American. For Tom, the question was moot, as he requested a friend from his hometown as his roommate. Unlike me, Tom was planning on a tennis career at Duke. When he visited Duke with his father, his dad had arranged a tennis game with one of the varsity players. After Tom split sets with the guy, his dad said, "I think you can make the team here."

Early in our first semester, Tom met Don Berns, a fellow engineering student and tennis player. Tom also connected quickly with Dr. James Bonk, the freshman chemistry teacher and volunteer assistant for the tennis team. Tom played with

Dr. Bonk a lot his freshman year, all fall and winter, I learned later. While I learned tennis on public courts, Tom learned the game at the local country club outside of St. Louis. He took lessons from Bill Price, who coached American stars Chuck McKinley and Jimmy Connors.

While Tom was hitting tennis balls with Dr. Bonk, I was playing pickup basketball games. Since Duke had a nationally ranked basketball team full of scholarship players, lots of good high school players, like me, were often competing in high-quality pickup games. These energetic basketball games helped me adjust to the challenges of college life.

Grades had always come easy for me in school until my first essay in the English composition course required of all freshmen. The graduate student leading my section asked us to explain the irony in a short story. I should have looked up the meaning of *irony* and thought the ideas through. He gave me a D. While I did get at least a C on my essays the rest of the semester, I felt humbled. Fortunately, classes involving numbers, calculus and physics, came easy for me, with mostly As on tests that first semester.

Besides feeling at home on the basketball court, I felt relaxed in my dorm, which had freshmen and upper classmen. I was scheduled to live in a triple room, but one guy went home after two days. The other guy spent his time in the library. I gravitated in my spare time to a room down the first-floor hall where three seniors lived. Two of the three were on their way to graduate school, one to be a doctor. But the third was worried about whether he would graduate. I studied hard that semester, determined to be like the first two. I learned how to iron shirts from the pre-med guy as we talked about basketball.

If sports talk was familiar, a newer experience awaited me. An upper classman introduced me to Roberta Flack's music. Duke only admitted its first black undergraduate students in 1963, two years before my entering class. As one of the first black students in this white university, he seemed relaxed and confident, on the exterior at least, happy to share his music with me and others. I felt comfortable in his room, learning about music. But I never got close enough to him to ask about where he grew up and how he experienced Duke. I was ready to be away from home but barely inching my way into big issues of the day – like the awkward beginnings of integration at Duke and in my life.

After my first Christmas vacation in college, we had another few weeks of class, then a study period before final exams. The semester system in most colleges worked that way in the 1960s. As the second semester began, tennis moved to the front of my mind. That 1965-66 academic year, freshmen were not eligible to play on varsity intercollegiate athletic teams. I thought I would have a good chance to make the freshman team.

The competition, however, looked intimidating – guys in white shirts and shorts reminded me of my nemesis in Jackson, Bill Hester, with smooth, well-grooved strokes. Tom Farquhar, a compact six-footer with a big serve, and tall, lanky Don Berns with a sweeping large forehand with full back-swing, looked like they would be hard to beat. I was a competitor, though, and worked for every point. Focused and intense, I won more challenge matches than I lost and finished in the top six. I made the team, one of the happy milestones of my freshman year.

I had missed competitive tennis my senior year in high school, after we moved away from Jackson. While we had a modest team at my high school, I had never found a tennis home in Nashville. This second semester of my freshman year, I found a base for my Duke years, a team of like-minded competitors. Basketball in the future held pickup games and intra-mural teams. But I was on a true college tennis team and was excited.

The freshmen team had only a few matches against nearby

schools. What was most exciting was simply being on the team. But one match stood out. We beat the University of North Carolina freshmen. Duke and UNC, only eight miles apart, have deep sports rivalries in football and basketball. But tennis was another matter. UNC had a long tradition of winning the Atlantic Coast Conference men's tennis championship. Duke had no tennis tradition, but our freshmen year brought a signature win, a great start to my new sports family.

Handball and Endorphins

In September of my sophomore year, Mike, my wrestler friend, and I moved into the same gothic dormitory where his brother had lived for three years, the Phi Kappa Sigma fraternity section. Athletes in football, basketball, and minor sports often joined this fraternity. Another Lake Junaluska friend, Bill Weldon – Alice's big brother – was a rising senior and a key member of the track team. In the adjoining dorm section, the Sigma Chi fraternity, Tom Farquhar and Don Berns settled into a double room. I felt right at home as my sophomore year began, surrounded by other athletes, childhood friends, and teammates.

Somehow, after upperclassmen chose their room in the Phi Kap dorm area, a single room on the third floor remained available. I thought about rooming with my buddy Mike but decided I would like the single room. As a bonus, the room was a few doors down the hall from Bill Weldon and his roommate, Ed Davis, who was beginning his applications to medical school. Through the fall and winter, I would wander down to their room for company, just as I had done with the upperclassmen my freshman year.

Trips to Bill and Ed's room gradually took on a dual role. I helped Bill with his economics class, which was difficult for him and came easy to me. Ed, in turn, introduced me to handball. Usually at night, sometimes as late as 11 p.m., he and I walked across the single road separating us from the athletic buildings to one of the two indoor handball courts. I was athletic, but Ed was a good handball player.

We would swat the small hard ball with our hands, protected only by a thin glove. He could find the coffin corner, as the shot is called, where the ball bounces off the front and a side wall almost at once and dies, virtually impossible to return. After an hour of streaking after low balls, stinging our hands over and over, we would walk back to the dorm, sweaty, exhausted, and exuberant, endorphins flowing through our bodies on clear North Carolina nights. We laughed and relived key shots. Carefree and happy to be alive.

Feeling the rush of endorphins from vigorous exercise, combined with feeling useful in helping Bill with economics and the easy-going conversations with these seniors, helped me stay grounded during the fall months. After the humbling experience in freshman English, I faced another issue my sophomore year. My courses were fine, easy to handle, mostly involving numbers and events – economics, accounting, and history. But I also took a psychology class where the instructor had us keep a dream diary. While I enjoyed learning about Freud and basic information in the field, the dream diary grabbed my interest in unexpected ways.

Dr. Kremen, the professor, had us keep a notebook at our bedside and asked us to immediately write down what we remembered when we woke up. Dutifully, I turned on the lamp beside my bed and scratched out whatever I could remember, free associating – phrases, images, people's names, random stuff. Later, looking for insights from this dream journal, no clear ideas emerged. Instead, the scribbles were confusing: people from Jackson, Lake Junaluska, Nashville, and now Duke tumbled together as if they knew each other. I appeared here and there but disappeared just as quickly. We did not discuss our dreams in Dr. Kremen's class beyond general points about dreams providing openings into our subconscious.

Routines pushed the dream notebooks out of my mind. Touch football games and pickup basketball games through the fall were always invigorating, now with the other athletes that were living in the same fraternity section. We also tended to eat together at the same two tables at the end of the large gothic cafeteria in the student union building. Classes and homework fell into an easy routine, no more stress of English essays. Despite these familiar patterns, when I returned to my dorm room, I found that my solitude could be lonely, even unnerving. With the novelty of freshman life over, I felt unsettled as a sophomore. The dreams seemed to highlight my being lost, not sure where I belonged. I did not discuss my dreams with Mike, Bill or Ed. The images remained unprocessed, raw data for buried treasure that I was not ready to pursue.

When languishing in my dorm room that fall, on a day with no endorphins firing from exercise, I would sometimes drift into a kind of numbness. I would lie on the single bed, on top of the old brown bedspread brought from home, with no energy or excitement about life. I was aware that something was lurking within me, an unsettled spirit that needed attention. But I had no idea what to do about it.

Psychology, Depression, a Book

Sitting now beside the new tennis center at my 50th anniversary, in 2019, I find my mind shifting from forehands and serves to psychology and depression. I smile, remembering that sophomore year in college with my dream diary. Alone in that single room, lying on top of the bedspread, I often felt lost and unhappy, sometimes numb, not feeling anything.

That fall of 1966, age 19, I had no idea that I was exhibiting a condition called dysthymia, a chronic low-grade depression. Often triggered by a significant change in life, dysthymia occurs when a person regularly feels moments of sadness, inertia, and hopelessness.

For me, writing a book helped me sort out dysthymia as a theme in my life: its recurrence at times of major transition and the ways I came to understand and address it in my mid-life years. My sophomore year at Duke was one of those times when dysthymia emerged from its lair. I did not have the tools to recognize or name my condition then, but I did have an invaluable way to help me cope with it – competitive tennis, as part of a team.

● 16 ●

My First Varsity Season

In 1967, as the second semester began, the tennis team had six weeks before our matches started. In the cold February afternoons and evenings, my hands dried until the skin on my thumb and forefinger cracked from gripping my racket for hours. I coated them with Vaseline at night. Then, back out again the next day, I wrapped my split skin with adhesive tape before hitting serves, practicing strokes, and playing challenge matches, which would decide our place on the team.

The coach, a physical education teacher and football coach, was near retirement. He mostly left us alone to work out our own practice routine. We hit and learned from each other or hitting with Dr. Bonk. Sometimes, however, our coach made an unexpected demand. One day, he decided that each of us had to be able to run a mile in less than six minutes. Fortunately, heavy exertion and sweating with pickup basketball games through the fall and winter put me in decent physical conditioning. But I was never a fast runner. Quick on the court, yes, but fleet on the track, not so much.

Our squad of about 10 players, more than half of us sophomores up from our successful freshman team, gathered at the track and stood at the starting line. I was among friends, all of us anxious for the matches to start in just a few weeks. Our coach held out his stopwatch and made the standard call: "On your mark, get set, go!"

Four laps around the track. I had watched many mile races at high school track meets but had never run one. Once around, fine. Second loop, I began to hurt and lagged as Tom and other better runners moved ahead. Third lap, painful. Starting the last lap, I ached, gasped, and felt my legs and lungs resisting as the coach called the time out. Just a couple of us were in this trailing group, trying to push through the last two turns to finish in under six minutes. I thought I might have to step onto the infield grass to throw up my lunch. Then I saw my friend Bill Weldon in the infield getting ready for his workout with the track team.

"Come on Bill, you can make it," he yelled at me, running along on the infield grass around the last curve. He kept yelling encouragement. My energy was sinking, my legs like rubber. Thank goodness for Bill Weldon. His familiar voice virtually dragged me to the finish line. His support made the difference. I made the six-minute mile and almost collapsed.

At the end of the pre-season competition, I secured the Number 6 singles slot. Tom and I played doubles together and landed the Number 3 spot. College matches have six flights of singles and three of doubles – in the 1960s, a total of nine points, one for each head-to-head match. I was delighted to be on the starting team and happy that I would not have to face the best players, those in the higher flights. Being on a college tennis team, a team in the Atlantic Coast Conference, felt like an honor. I was proud to be in this group of guys about to compete for the school up and down the East coast.

A jam-packed stretch of seven weeks awaited us. The matches finally began on Monday, March 20, on our home courts against Ohio State. A great day for tennis, overcast, around 70 degrees. In trim white shorts and shirt, my Duke jacket with the crossed tennis rackets on the logo, I stepped into my varsity career. At 2 p.m., the six flights of singles headed out for the best of three sets. Our coach called the names from the list on his clipboard. First flight, "Bruce

Mahler for Duke," he said, handing him a can of new balls. Bruce joined the top Ohio State player, and they stepped just a few steps away onto court 1, right in front of us. Bruce, a junior and a wizard with a racket, was a nationally ranked badminton player from New England.

I waited patiently for my name to be called as flight after flight headed down the freshly cleared clay courts. One after the other, the six zones, each with that clear demarcation of a webbed net, awaited a unique combination of artistry and combat about to unfold. Our senior captain, Fred Turner, moved out to the number 2 court, and then the four sophomores heard our names called one after the other: Don Berns for court 3, Tom Farquhar for flight 4, Charles Meek down to court 5, and finally, I got my new can of balls, met my opponent, and walked outside the fence down past the other courts to number 6. At last, my college varsity career would begin. I was happy, excited, doing what I had loved since my early years in Mississippi.

Walking past the other courts, my friends warming up for their first varsity match, I felt a tingle hearing the thwop of the ball coming off the racket, then a pause, and another thwop from the other side of the net. Muscles were getting warm, the nerves of this new stage of my tennis life attuned to sounds and silences. I could almost taste an early spring flavor of new life blowing from the early blossoms across the street.

Then we reached distant court 6 and began our warmup. I was heartened to realize that I could beat this guy if I played the way I had been hitting in practice, winning enough challenge matches to land this varsity position. In that first set nerves did not calm down right away, leading to unforced errors, including double faults. Less than an hour into my varsity career, I was down a set. But I steadied myself, gave my flat forehands a little more "air" to clear the net, and focused hard on getting my serve in. I took the second set, then pulled away in the third for the win. I smiled and gulped water on the walk back to the coaches' area by court 1. Fresh orange slices gave me the juice I needed to revive for the doubles round. Tom and I won easily at the number 3 doubles flight. Duke won all six singles matches, plus our doubles for a 7-2 victory over the Big Ten school. A great start to the season.

The spring semester now felt like a sprint, with 17 matches jammed into seven weeks. Our first week, we played four matches on our home courts, Monday through Thursday. Each day, exhausted by singles and doubles, we would shower, grab dinner, and finish homework. Up the next day for morning classes, an early lunch and back out to a 2 p.m. match. Our first two matches were convincing wins, and my confidence as a college tennis player was beginning to grow. *I belong at this level*. But late in the week, I got a dose of humility as two strong teams beat us handily. My first week's record in singles and doubles was two wins, two losses. I felt satisfied with this start.

Learn from It

Friday, March 24, 1967, after morning classes, seven players, along with our head coach and Dr. Bonk, climbed into two cars and headed to Florida for spring break. First stop, Clemson, South Carolina, where we would play our first ACC match. Clemson had begun to give scholarships and recruit, going beyond the States for a couple of foreign players. We feared being overmatched but thought we would have a shot, at least winning a few matches. We were not going to roll over to the Clemson Tigers; they were going to have to beat us. And they did, taking all nine matches.

After our three matches in Florida, two easy wins and a loss, we stopped at the University of South Carolina on the way home for our second ACC match. They beat us easily.

After nine matches in thirteen days and the round-trip drive to Florida, we were exhausted and ready to be home. I hunkered down in my single room with accounting problems, European history readings, and French vocabulary. With my psych class over, I no longer kept a dream diary. Tom and Don were back in their double room in the adjacent Sigma Chi fraternity section, with their various engineering courses. We had the entire week off for light practices and resting our bodies.

We came back into action with a couple of easy wins and a loss to a strong Presbyterian College team. I won one of Duke's two points that day in a long, tight singles match. A week later, we went to Chapel Hill and played the perennial ACC powerhouse and Duke's rival in all sports, the University of North Carolina (UNC).

Six soft clay courts were nestled among tall pines on the picturesque campus. Their coach had been at Chapel Hill for many years and was known for tough practices and good recruiting. I was nervous heading down to the far end court, away from the small crowd that had turned out. Even for the best team in the conference, this minor sport attracted only die-hard tennis fans. My opponent hit smooth strokes on both sides, not overpowering pace but consistent and deep shots landing near the baseline. I had noticed he was scheduled to play on their number 1 doubles team, paired with the no. 1 UNC singles player. *He must have a good net game as well, I* thought as we warmed up.

He hit virtually every shot in the court, no unforced errors, as the announcers these days label shots that I was, unfortunately, hitting way too often. He beat me handily. Only Charles Meek, our number 5 player, managed to win a set from the mighty Tar Heels.

As the season wound down, the team record stood at 6-7. We all wanted to end at least 50-50 for the season, if possible. We had three ACC head-to-head matches in four days with travel squeezed in. Little time for schoolwork or to catch our collective and competitive breath. First up, Wake Forest, in Durham, on Saturday, April 29.

In doubles, Tom and I split the first two sets and, after a long day of tennis, began the deciding third set. We realized that the other two doubles matches were over and that the team score stood at four matches each. Everyone stood and watched us in the deciding set for an ACC victory. We stayed aggressive, trying to take over the net as much as we could. But neither our efforts nor our teammates' encouragement was enough. Dr. Bonk offered good advice to our disappointment: "Don't worry about it too much. Learn from it."

The next day, Sunday, we drove to College Park, Maryland, in time to rest before our final ACC matches, scheduled for the next two days. On Monday, we played the University of Maryland. After the match, we drove two hours south to Charlottesville, Virginia.

On Tuesday, we played our final ACC match against the University of Virginia. Both matches were close, up and down the flights of singles and doubles.

In both the Maryland and Virginia matches, Tom and I won a critical point at number 3 doubles as teammates watched and cheered. Dr. Bonk's advice served us well. Duke pulled out both matches, five to four. I was proud to be part of those victories. The disappointment of the Wake Forest loss had not triggered despondency, that numbness that would visit me in my single dorm room. The tennis season was giving me joy and supporting a healthy state of mind. I was playing for more than myself. Maybe that was the key: playing for the team.

On May 5, 1967, the mighty University of Miami team stepped onto the Duke courts, part of a trip that would take them to the UNC courts the next day. Jamie Fillol from Chile played number 1; he was expected to become a touring professional. (Seven years later, Fillol was ranked No. 14 in the world.) I started strong against the sixth-best Miami player, winning a long, hard first set 8-6. (The "tiebreaker," now used when a set reaches 6-6, had not yet entered mainstream tennis.) While I stayed focused and played well, he played better, winning two close sets. After a short break, Tom and I took the court to play the Number 3 doubles match.

Tom served first as he always did for us and held. I managed to hold my serve throughout the first set as well. Tom, as usual, played on the left side of the court, the "ad" side, where he could hit his strong backhand. I played the deuce court on the right where I could hit more forehands, my best shot. We were fearless, playing a team that, on paper, should beat us handily. We broke Miami once to take the first set 7-5. Miami took the close second set. After well over four hours of tennis, first a long three-set singles match and then a split-set doubles match, I took deep breaths and drank more water. One more set. Tom served better than ever, and I held my serve too. We took the close third set at 6-4. Miami did not skunk us that day. That was the best day Tom and I had on the doubles court at Duke.

After the Miami loss, Duke had one last shot at evening our record. But our last match was canceled because of rain, so we ended our season with an overall record of 8-9, 3-4 in the conference. Only the ACC tournament was left, held in 1967 on our Duke courts.

On the first day of the three-day event, the eight ACC teams arrived along with a downpour. Matches would have to be crammed together in two days. UNC and Clemson had by far the strongest teams that year, with South Carolina a distant third. The other five teams followed, all with similar records: Maryland, Virginia, Duke, Wake Forest, and NC State.

In singles, the number 6 flight, I was seeded sixth but upset the number 3 seed Maryland player in the first round. Then, in the winner's bracket, I lost to a strong Clemson player in the semifinals but won the match for third place. Tom and I also finished third in our doubles flight. We were proud of our year, with third in the conference and our win over Miami. Duke had three third-place finishes, my singles and doubles, and Charlie Meek at the number 5 singles flight. Duke placed fifth in the conference tournament, edging the same teams we beat during the season – Maryland, Virginia, and NC State.

Lessons from Winning

Sitting at the modern tennis center, with 50th reunion events around the campus underway, I let moments from my early years at Duke bounce about in my head like well-hit forehands. The overhead sun prompts a light moisture under my shirt, reminding me of those sweat-soaked tennis shirts. The courts were like home, the balls shooting across the net as bits of clay popped up to dirty my white shoes. And I remember that first ACC tournament, held right here, draw sheets spread about, the dramas in each flight of matches unfolding. I smile.

That tournament, really my entire sophomore year, was when I learned what winning felt like. A combination of skill, strategy, and training led to the wins over Miami and in the ACC tournament. Another key ingredient also evolved over the season – confidence, in my game and in myself. A belief in self. I felt I belonged on a tennis court with other good players. The courts were my home.

As I relaxed into being my best self on the court at age 20, winning became a habit. Playing next to Tom helped me learn these lessons. Many times, already tired after a singles match, sometimes a disheartening loss, I would go back on the court and start again in doubles. Then, working with Tom, we knew we would each make errors as well as great shots. We played the match as a team. Through it all, the mental strain was more demanding than the physical.

Tom always seemed wise for his years. His sister was born deaf, and he had developed a more sensitive awareness of the world than most young college students. Plus, he had made the hard choice to quit lessons from a legendary tennis teacher in St. Louis because he loved to play basketball as well. Whatever made Tom the confident person he was that sophomore year, his sense of knowing who he was gradually carried over to me. I was beginning to learn how to feel.

● 17 ●

Changing Times

After the excitement of my first ACC tournament, our tight group of four sophomores on the tennis team dispersed to the last weeks of classes, a reading period and exams. Tom and Don tackled their engineering exams. Charlie Meek had ROTC exercises, which helped pay his way through Duke. I was a disciplined student and reviewed notes systematically. Not so great at French despite lots of hours in the language lab, listening to conversations over headphones. But I got through the language requirement fine. Exams were no great burden.

We went our separate ways for the summer. Tom and Don had formed a unique bond, almost like brothers. Roommates and engineering students, both from the Midwest. They planned on seeing each other during the summer and playing a lot of tennis. Charlie would head back to his home in Oklahoma between school and required ROTC summer training.

With the season and then the semester over, I reached the halfway point in my college experience. Now 20 years old, I did not spend the summer at Lake Junaluska, my first time away from that cocoon of friendships and family since I was a young child.

One of my fraternity brothers at Duke had worked at a large YMCA sailing camp for years and told me they needed someone to run their tennis program. The land activities were considered unimportant at this sea-oriented camp, but I was still thrilled to get the job. I would set up a tennis program from scratch – literally, scratching out the service lines and baselines, putting plumblines down before spreading the lime to recreate the four dirt courts used the previous summer. Then, putting up the net posts, hanging the nets, and sorting out the rackets in storage, ready for another season of teaching boys how to play tennis.

Assisting me were a college and a high school student, both avid tennis players, thrilled to be working with a major college tennis guy. Seen through the summer as a role model on the court reinforced my confidence as a tennis player and as a person. Instead of the guy playing at number 6, the bottom of the roster, I was their star. A real tennis player.

At the end of the season, the college assistant and I found a good court in a nearby town and played a match. He was happy to win a few games, and I was delighted to see that my time on the courts over the summer, even as I hit endless balls to beginning and intermediate players, had helped my basics – watch the ball, prepare early for strokes, move my feet.

With several weeks before the fall semester began, I drove south to Savannah, Georgia, to visit with the family of one of the doctors who came to the sailing camp. During my visit, coincidentally, there was a tennis tournament in town that attracted excellent players from several states. I entered with no expectations and drew the top seed, a tall, lanky guy who played number 1 at Clemson. I remembered him, but I doubt if he knew me, way down in the sixth flight on one of the weaker teams in the conference. Instead of worrying about being overwhelmed by a superior player, I relaxed, incorporating my carefree approach to tennis over the summer. I walked out onto the clay court with no socks, dressed as I did at camp, my legs tanned all the way to my shoe tops.

With the doctor and his kids cheering me on, I stepped into the first set fearlessly. My shots went hard into the corners, and I hustled to the net to crack winning volleys. I jumped ahead, to my surprise, and a crowd started to form, seeing the top seed in trouble. I kept playing great, but he began to put pressure on me; my magical run ended with a close loss in the first set. He moved through the second set easily for the win. Even with the loss, I played one of my best matches since I took a set from Bill Hester in my junior year in high school. I walked away feeling like a winner.

Growing Up

Sitting at the Duke tennis courts now, 52 years after that tournament in Savannah, I slowly stand up and stretch. Maybe 30 minutes of real time have passed since I left the athletes' reception, but decades-old images have flashed across my internal computer screen. The third-place finish in the ACC tournament, dirt courts at Camp Sea Gull, and my sockless performance against one of the strongest opponents of my entire tennis career.

Other images are not as clear. What life lessons were beginning to come into focus by my junior year? How did I see the world at age 20, with the adult world after college within sight? Across the parking lot stands the same gothic dormitory where I lived my last years at Duke. In 1964, I started my junior year, not long after Bob Dylan alerted us to the changing times and to the answers blowing in the wind.

The academic load awaiting me offered some guidance. In my religion class, the book of Isaiah started to make some sense, even Old Testament talk of the Messiah. A member of a prominent string quartet in Durham led a music survey course with the devotion of a ministry. American history came alive with the popular young teacher Ann Scott. Curiosity and learning began to take hold. College became more than completing assignments. A few economics and business courses held their charm; working with numbers always relaxed me, and the courses were sufficient to avoid having to change majors my junior year. Now though, I wanted to read more books and express my thoughts through writing.

In history, Dr. Scott asked us to imagine what role our families would have played in the times of slavery. She encouraged the single African American student in our class to share his thoughts. I was impressed by his courage, speaking to a room full of white students. I lacked the confidence to share much in that class, not sure what I felt about the privilege I would have had in antebellum times. In 1967, even Ann Scott was not emphasizing the narrative of white privilege that dominated the Duke landscape: virtually all students and faculty, White; virtually all janitors, cafeteria workers, and grounds workers, Black. Even if the term "white privilege" was not yet in the air, I began to shift from a childhood numbness to segregation to an unsettledness now stirring in a 20-year-old.

Where I was more comfortable with my impulses was the basketball court. Now familiar with the many good basketball players in our fraternity and beyond, I spent a lot of time in the gym. Our fraternity fielded two strong teams in the intramural tournament. Our "B" team, better and our senior-led "A" team, reached the finals. The Kappa Alpha team, our opponent, was too strong, led by 6-foot, 5-inch Al Woodall, the Duke football quarterback that year. The runner-up place in a school loaded with great basketball players was my best ever in the sport and a good send-off into my second year of varsity tennis.

Still my emotional energy lapsed when not engaged with my academic load or stimulated in the gym. Much later in life, I would understand I was fending off dysthymia, tucking it away into some patchwork of emotional threads. Sports, friends, and learning mostly pulled me through this fabric. But at times, I needed more. Therapy and antidepressants were years into the future. I needed help to understand and move through the darkness. Alas, no more handball now that

Ed was gone to medical school. No more comfort from my old friend Bill Weldon. But I did have a tennis team.

Tennis, an Anchor

In the spring of 1968, we had only two home matches before heading to Florida, where we played four more times. Because of my success as a sophomore, the coach put me at number 3 singles, where I played much tougher opponents than my sophomore year and mostly lost. Tom and I still played number 3 doubles, but he was not the same player as the year before. The summer after our sophomore year, he was sick in bed for six weeks. Coming back to school, he did not regain his coordination and dropped out of the regular rotation for singles. He also had mononucleosis during the spring, limiting his energy. After nine matches in three weeks, I was discouraged by my singles losses, and we were struggling in doubles. But suddenly, a much bigger challenge arose.

On Thursday afternoon, April 4, we had an easy practice day. That evening, Dr. Martin Luther King Jr. was assassinated in Memphis. The next night, I joined about 500 students who walked from the main campus to the home of the Duke University president. The leaders of the march took demands to the president regarding cafeteria workers, who were seeking a wage increase, and issues related to black students and faculty. Events dovetailed, leading to what became known as the Vigil, held on the large lawn area in front of the Duke Chapel. The Vigil consumed the Duke campus for about 10 days, where students, mostly White and privileged, honored King while also supporting the cafeteria workers' demand for a $1.60 an hour wage. Some also focused on growing demands among black students for more attention to their needs on campus, including more black faculty.

Despite approaching my 21st birthday and having grown

up in the racial cauldron of Jackson, Mississippi, I was not ready to sort out a political stance. Some impulse did push me into that first march to the president's house, but I left with about half the crowd after the first round of speeches. Many marchers stayed all night pressing their demands, welcomed by the sympathetic president. As the Vigil took hold, hundreds of people eventually spread across the muddy field in front of the Chapel, under umbrellas and makeshift tarp covers. People were boycotting classes and the dining hall, sitting in the quad.

Walking by the Vigil about the third day in, one of the organizers stopped me. "Bill, will you call your father and ask him to endorse the Vigil? It would be great to have a Methodist bishop support it." He caught me totally off guard. I barely knew him, and I didn't know how I felt about joining the Vigil.

"No, I won't call him." I was surprised by my sharp, sudden reply. "You can call him yourself." He looked startled, probably expecting a sympathetic ear. If I had had more confidence, maybe more patience, I would have asked him to help me understand the Vigil. How would staying away from classes help the cafeteria workers? But he was not interested in me, only an endorsement from my father. I needed someone to be interested in me, even if I had white privilege.

I felt confused and overwhelmed by the events unfolding. I figured my father was paying my tuition for me to go to classes, not to skip them. I was still going to class.

Three days into the Vigil, about the time Joan Baez showed up, along with national news crews, we had a match with North Carolina State. I went to the tennis courts for refuge and to be responsible, to meet my commitment to the team. And to escape the complex world of changing times. Maybe tennis kept me from plunging into self-reflection about race and protest, about making a political statement of support for underpaid black cafeteria workers and underrepresented black students and faculty. Or maybe tennis gave me a life-line, a home, and self-confidence. I knew what I was doing on the court, even when I was losing more matches than I won. I knew the rules of engagement.

A Race in Maryland

The 1968 Atlantic Coast Conference tennis tournament was the worst performance of the Duke University tennis team during my years there. We lost to a variety of strong and weak players through the six singles and three doubles flights. Our confidence as individuals and as a team slowly slipped away through the painful, three-day ordeal. Tom and I were dead last in the number 3 doubles flight; I squeaked by in my last match against the NC State player for seventh in the number 3 singles flight. Overall, Duke fell to seventh place in the tour-nament, edging out the woefully weak NC State team.

With a few hours left before the five-hour drive home to Durham, North Carolina, our season over, Tom suggested a diversion – a 100-yard dash.

"We'll feel better. Come on Fingo," Tom said, using my nickname among the tennis team. This was a bad idea. I knew it. But I went with my tribe, the guys I played tennis with every afternoon that spring, my closest friends at Duke.

We headed over to the nearby track that circled the foot-ball field, made of fine cinders, popular for 1960s-vintage tracks. Four of us lined up as if in a race for the gold. We could have put on our tennis nametag handles: Fingo, Farqo, Sacko, and Bernie – aka, the doubles team of Bill and Tom, Chuck Saacke (our best player), and tall Don Berns.

Two speedy teammates moved ahead quickly – Farqo and Sacko, the two best athletes among us. They stretched their lead. I hit my first wall at about 30 yards. *One hundred yards is a very long sprint for a tennis player*, I was thinking. They moved further ahead, and the finish line finally came into view. I glanced over at Bernie and saw the sweat beading on his face, grimacing. I reached deeper into my memory of sprinters at Murrah High School, remembering gazelles floating or pounding the track in Jackson, Mississippi, with announcers saying things like, "Here come the big fellow and the little guy."

Long and lanky, six feet, four-inch Don Berns and I chased Tom and Chuck from the rear, hip by hip on the cinder track in College Park, Maryland. Our fastest teammates crossed the finish line and leaned over to catch their breath. My nagging doubt about this race surged with maybe 20 yards left. Don's long strides sounded steady against the loose track pebbles while I grunted and groaned trying to push my skinny legs forward.

We needed a commentator: "Here come Fingo and Bernie, side by side. The tall, smooth racehorse a nose ahead of the kid struggling to keep up." The announcer might gasp for air. Then... "Finger is struggling, Berns is edging ahead. He has a bit more left. But wait, Finger's left hand is moving toward the tall guy." The commentator's voice grows louder, a bit frantic even. "Wait... I can't believe it. Finger pushed Berns in the shoulder. He's lost his balance, Berns is crashing onto the cinder track."

Fingo finished a distant third behind Socko and Farqo. Bernie righted himself from the cinder track eventually, glared at Fingo and yelled a little. He limped back toward the tennis courts where we would soon get in the two cars and drive back to Durham. But Don was too sore to drive his car that day. Tom had to drive for him.

Too Hard on Yourself

In that race, I felt small in stature and spirit, as I did many days that spring of 1968. There I was with my friend and teammate, who, for that moment, became my mortal enemy. My psyche could not take another loss. Fear must have laid deep in my belly, somehow, perhaps fear about life ahead. Or, more specifically, maybe the nagging fear of going to Vietnam, where my lifelong friend Bill Weldon was now stationed. Whatever the source, I was guided that day less by stamina than by self-doubt, frustration, sadness, and grief. My body did not settle into a relaxed pace of love and friendship with my friend Don, who always seemed to smile even when racing down a cinder track in Maryland.

I required so much from my tennis matches at Duke those four years, from this game, from this tribe. I didn't even know what I was asking. But somehow, my closest friend, Farquhar, had led me to a showdown on this track, now a place of danger, not respite. Maybe the grief of the world was somehow finding me in this race, the pain of racism from my Mississippi make-up, deep in my heritage and psyche.

Whatever was driving my body that day, some dark instinct may have emerged. I'm not sure what happened at the finish line. I was too young a man, still a child really, to incorporate the combination of joy and sorrow that tennis brought me. White privilege gave me the opportunity to discover the game of tennis on the public clay courts at Battlefield Park in Jackson. More white privilege got me to Duke and helped make tennis a lifelong anchor.

Somehow this track race in 1968 seemed to be asking me to grow up now, to accept my place in this human race. This was a race for my life, but I did not have the tools I needed that day. Only instincts of survival were functioning.

More than 50 years after this race, I show my write-up to Tom, the only other witness still alive. "I think you're being too hard on yourself," he says. "I think it was more of a slip for Don. You might have brushed against him a little. But I don't think you pushed him."

The last time I saw Don was a Duke reunion, maybe our

30th. Tom and I hit a few tennis balls. Don sat in the old bleachers – the new stadium not yet erected. We all ate lunch together. His Parkinson's disease had advanced significantly, with symptoms that severely affected his gross motor skills. He was still trim and smiling, his large frame jerking from side to side as he held onto his walker.

I never heard a harsh word from Don, not even after our race debacle in Maryland. Sure, he had a few reactions after finding himself on the track, but even then, Don was guided more by empathy than revenge. He trained to be an engineer but was always a people person. Soon after college, he became a Presbyterian minister and worked with youth for many years, even after his diagnosis. Don Berns was a kind man and a good tennis player. I'm sorry I never knew him better. I miss him.

Tennis gave me a group of friends, an anchor every after-noon. In 1968, we talked mostly about tennis, not about the Vigil or the Vietnam War protests, which had made their way onto our campus. In our posed photo that spring, these well-groomed young white men with short haircuts wore white zipped tennis jackets with the Duke logo on the chest. The three on the front row held wooden Wilson Jack Kramer rack-ets across their torsos. I'm on the back row next to sophomore Chuck Saacke, who had a movie star grin. Tom is on my other side, looking grim, maybe realizing this would be a tough year for him. The leaves are just starting to come out on the trees in the background. My junior season was just about to begin.

Visible behind us is my dorm, and beyond, at the top of the photo, the large clock on the spire of the student union building. It's 3:50 on a practice day. The cafeteria workers have started cooking the evening meal in the large gothic dining hall below the clock tower. I will eat there in several hours after practice, making my way to the end of the hall where the Phi Kap fraternity members sit and swap tales. Where some of us in April tentatively discussed the Vigil, like why we were not boycotting the cafeteria or classes.

Now, in 2019, I head toward the book exhibit in the modern student union building. The cobblestone walkways through the quadrangles of dormitories are worn in areas that gather water after rainstorms. Even after decades, the slabs of uneven stone still seem familiar from trips back and forth from the student union and classes to the dorm and tennis. At the same time, now in my 70s, this walk seems as distant as a foreign country, like European cobblestones.

As I leave the last quadrangle of dorms, the walkway opens up to a small plaza. I skirt the old student union and head straight for the Bryan Center. The multi-level building houses student support services, a performing arts theater and exhibition venues. In a large reception area, volunteers are directing reunion participants to various activities.

● 18 ●

Away from Tennis

Twenty-six members of the Duke University class of 1969 have books displayed around a spacious room on the main floor of the Bryan Center. The exhibit includes up to four books for each author, along with personal statements presented on poster boards. A small booklet contains a summary of the exhibit, the author statements, and a bibliography for those with more than four works. The booklet notes that the 26 graduates include "prolific and prize-winning authors, as well as some who began writing after another career."

I find my book on the back wall across from the entrance to the room and stare at the handsome cover: *The Crane Dance: Taking Flight in Midlife* by William R. Finger. The book evolved over many years, finding focus through stories from my 40s and early 50s. In that midlife period, I learned how depression operated in my life as I gradually harnessed tools to forge a new way of living. The whooping crane became a metaphorical talisman for me during this period; nearing extinction, this magnificent stately bird made a comeback thanks to hard work by many rescuers and advocates. I identified with the whooping crane, which survived and began to flourish.

I pick up the book and feel its heft. My hand seems to find the page when I always smile. Inspired by the Karate Kid movie, I wrote, "I start doing little crane dances to accent my long, thin arms as huge wings, my hands bent at the wrist, fingers pointing down." I described my lean legs, balancing, bending, jumping as my arms flapped. "As I practice in the backyard, I feel as though I'm soaring through my imagination."

Standing alone in the large room now, no others around, I feel a huge sense of accomplishment. At the same time, walking slowly through the exhibit, I pause to admire the multiple books by those who made a career of publishing books, some freelancers with established publishing houses and others through academic careers. One person who had played on the freshman tennis team had produced documentary films for a living.

I chuckle reading one personal statement. "I got a C in Freshman English at Duke," wrote Vince Staten. "I was a math major until I took a Screenwriting course at That Nameless College Ten Miles Away and got an A." After graduating and "sitting around waiting to be drafted," this math major landed a news job in Tennessee and kept writing. He's published 15 books, shared an editor with Harper Lee, and had six different editors at Simon & Schuster. "If there is a lesson in this, it's don't worry about a C in freshman English. It has nothing to do with becoming a writer."

My hopes of publishing books as a livelihood never materialized. But I did work as a writer and editor for 35 years – as a freelancer, at a public policy center for a decade, and then for an international public health research organization for 24 years. I too did not worry about my C in English.

Still, reading the summary statements and admiring the other books, I feel a little like being number 6 on a college tennis team, even one with no scholarship players. I was a good player and won some tough matches, but there were so many who were better, more accomplished, more successful. I know that such comparative thinking can bring me down from this moment of pride, looking at my book. I am one of 26 authors in a class of several thousand graduates from an outstanding university. Most importantly, writing *The Crane Dance* helped me understand the sources of my dysthymia and how I moved to a new phase of life. Maybe it will help others who get a chance to read it.

On this spring day in 2019, 50 years after graduating from college, I notice something new about my life story. At age 40, just as I entered the midlife period covered in *The Crane Dance*, I stopped playing tournament tennis. Then, at age 70, shortly after I published *The Crane Dance*, tennis again took on a central role in my life. With the book written, published, and promoted, space fell open for me to return to one of the most joyful places in my childhood, the tennis court.

Questions remain about this 30-year gap in my tennis career, from age 40 to 70. While tennis offered a refuge during difficult times, did it also keep me from coming to terms with central psychological, even spiritual, issues in my life? To grapple with the core enigma of my life, did I need time away from tennis, away from this coping tool, one might call it? And, depending on the answers to these questions, what role is tennis playing for me now in my 70s, with depression no longer a challenge in my life?

Tennis in Europe

During the spring of 1968, Tom, Don, Chuck Saacke, and I – the quartet that would end that tennis season with our infamous cinder-track race – began to talk about a possible trip to Europe over the summer. Tom had traveled with his family over the years and knew how to work with a travel agent. "We can do this Fingo," he said. "Let's go to Europe!"

Except for a Boy Scout Jamboree at age 12 in Colorado, when I traveled by bus with a bunch of young scouts and leaders from Mississippi, I had never been out of the South, much less to Europe. But my brother had studied in Germany during college and was there again on a year abroad. I was game to go across the ocean and came across a notice of a tournament in Bristol, England. It was one of the main "warm-up" tournaments for Wimbledon, the most famous tennis venue in the world.

I wrote the tournament director – this was long before email or easy trans-Atlantic calls – asking if she would accept four members of the Duke University tennis team. To our shock, she welcomed us and also offered train fare from London with food and lodging in Bristol. When the invitation arrived, I jumped with excitement outside the postbox area in the Student Union. We were going to Bristol, England, to play on grass courts with some of the best players in the world. Tom worked with a travel agent to get us cheap tickets on Icelandic Airlines. We planned to go first to the tournament and then rent a VW van for a month-long ramble around Europe.

As badly as our second varsity season ended on that Maryland track, we had become good friends over the years on the court. Exams over, we went to our separate homes with plans to meet at Kennedy Airport to wedge ourselves into those tight seats aboard Icelandic Air. Our overnight flight was scheduled for the night of June 6, 1968.

Early the morning of June 5, I left Lake Junaluska in western North Carolina, driving the little red VW bug my brother had given me when he took off for Europe the previous summer. I planned to get on the interstate and let the I-95 signs guide me up the East Coast. As soon as I got in range of a good radio station, I started looking for music to keep me company. But what I found was news of Robert Kennedy being shot shortly after midnight in Los Angeles after winning the California primary. All day up I-95, I heard updates on Kennedy's condition. The news got worse as I moved through Richmond and Washington, around Baltimore and finally onto the New

Jersey Turnpike. I managed to get through Manhattan and onto my great-uncle's house in southern Connecticut.

The next day, my great-uncle took me to Kennedy Airport. Robert Kennedy's death early that morning as we slept left a pall over the ride. Boarding the Icelandic flight with my tennis teammates, tennis racket and knapsack in hand, I pushed the Kennedy news into that cave in my psyche that could not process more grief and confusion about the world.

By the time we arrived in Luxembourg, I was tired and sore from the cramped seats, but my eyes were agog at this new place called Europe, outdoor patio seating around cobblestones older than our country. I had no idea what to order for lunch as the waitress held her pencil at the ready. "Just order a ham and cheese sandwich," Tom said. "They have those here." Tom was comfortable as our guide, drawing on his experience and a few books we had brought.

Later that day, on a train through Luxembourg to Belgium and across the French countryside, I couldn't sleep. When we finally reached the port town of Calais for our ferry ride to the famed white cliffs of Dover, we learned that no ferries were operating. In fact, much of France had ground to a halt with major student uprisings.

"We have to get to London tonight," I managed in my college French to various port officials. But no one seemed to care. Finally, a taxi driver noticed me tugging at my wallet.

"I drive you over border to Belgium," he said. "Ferry there." The four of us piled in. "Watch Andre in his Citroen." The car zoomed forward. "I drive as good as New York, yes?"

During a four-hour night ride at a 100-kilometer clip, he hardly slowed down through small villages along the way. More than once that night my heart leapt higher than my throat, cutting off what I thought would be my last gasp. Somehow, Andre maneuvered his way past real and my imagined barriers and took us safely to the Belgian dock.

We hit the spectacular cliffs at dawn. After navigating Victoria Station in London, we found the train to Bristol. No time for a stroll along the Thames. The others dozed. But the English countryside absorbed me with pastoral scenes of sheep and thatched roofs.

"We've been expecting you," the Bristol tournament director said as we reached the tennis venue. His efficient singsong of a greeting was a welcome sound to my U.S. ears. "Make yourselves at home. Teatime is just ending. At the social desk, you can learn the families you're staying with. Excuse me, I have to talk to Mr. Ashe." I glanced across the room to see Arthur Ashe.

I found a chair near a pile of shortbread cookies and chicken salad sandwiches. We had not eaten a meal since the continent. I poured a large glass of orange soda. "Boy, this is strong," I said to no one in particular.

"You've finished the whole bottle?" a passing waitress asked with a bewildered look. Then she started chuckling. "You're an American aren't you? I bet you've never been to England before."

"How did you know?" I asked, disguising what was left of my Mississippi drawl after three years at Duke.

"That's concentrate, dearie," she said in a Cockney twang. "We mix it with water for orange squash. It should've lasted you the afternoon." I laughed politely. "But you've got spirit. I'll bring you another and some more sandwiches."

That night my host wanted to hear about our tennis and travels. Before finally sleeping, I tried to explain that I lacked the experience of the Flying Dutchman, Tom Okker, their guest the previous year, who had won many world-class tournaments. "George Washington slept here" adds a touch of charm at USA tourist stops, but I can't say that "Okker slept here" gave me more confidence as I was about to play with the likes of Arthur Ashe the next day.

The Dream of Wimbledon

The next day, I dressed slowly in the locker room. Herb FitzGibbon stood nearby, getting ready for our match. A former Princeton star, he was currently No. 14 in the United States and a regular competitor on the international circuit. Walking out to the No. 1 stadium court, I felt relaxed. "Nothing to lose," I kept telling myself.

We spun a racket on the soft grass beside the umpire's chair to determine who would serve first. I won. Then we warmed up. FitzGibbon's strokes came off the grass like artillery fire. The ball skidded so fast, I swung quickly, almost blindly just to hit the ball at all. But I adjusted quickly, and my shots began spinning back.

"Begin play," the umpire announced. "Ball girls ready?" He looked to the corners of the court, priming the schoolgirls. "Players ready?" I nodded, as cool as the grass on an early morning.

I walked back to the baseline and bounced the ball twice on the mush of grass. I had decided to hit both serves as hard as I could, forgoing the caution of spinning my second serve. I boomed the first toward FitzGibbon's forehand; he lunged and missed. "Fault," barked the umpire. I aimed the second at the same spot and found the corner. "Fifteen-love," the official said. I kept up the strategy through the first game. FitzGibbon got two serves back, but I hit my return strokes as hard as I could.

"Mr. Finger leads the first set, one game to love," announced the gentleman in the chair.

FitzGibbon looked me over more closely when we crossed sides of the court, as if he had missed something in the locker room. Then he bounced the ball at the baseline before pounding his own first serves in – 15. 30. 40. Game.

"One game all, first set."

A few spectators scattered about the courts caught a glimpse of our match. Most were bunched across the stadium at court No. 2. But when the umpire announced that I had won the third game – "Mr. Finger leads two games to one, first set" – people started moving toward our side. Fans who were following the draw knew FitzGibbon was highly regarded, and the winner of our match would play Ashe.

As the crowd began stirring, upset in the air, my serves began missing. His bombardment of shots from across the net found their mark again and again. I blasted a few more winning serves but could not sustain rallies.

"Mr. FitzGibbon wins the first set, 6 games to 2. Mr. Finger serving first game, second set."

A last ounce of hope propelled my first four serves into corners. Again, I took the lead for the set. But the fans had left by the middle of the second set, going for a squash or to watch a closer match. Only sunbathers, early arrivals, and our hosts' teenage daughter remained.

Through the second set, I soaked in the moments, knowing my grandchildren would benefit someday from the story. Shaking FitzGibbon's hand, I felt no humiliation with a 6-2, 6-1 defeat. I felt even better the next day when FitzGibbon pushed Ashe to the limit before the slender American star won. A few years later, Ashe would win Wimbledon.

I tangled with the best and had my nose rubbed in the grass. But at least for a single day, I shared a locker room and the courts with the best in the world.

Summer Awakening

We returned to the continent and were happy to tuck our rackets into a safe crevice of our rented VW van. From Amsterdam, we began our trip around the continent. In Paris, we hit a few museums, Notre Dame, Montmartre, a girlie show, and one additional suggestion from me, a bow to my music appreciation course. Walking the streets one evening, I guided us to the famous Paris opera house, a magnificent building dating from Napoleon's reign in the 19th century.

The four of us bounced through our first several weeks with carefree exuberance, looking for mounds of spaghetti in Italy and beer steins in Munich. Some days, I walked on European streets wondering what I was doing there, a shade of despondency entering my gait. But the next sightseeing adventure would pick me up again, and I'd get immersed in some castle in Austria or gondola in Venice or beer hall in Germany. The weeks raced by as we spun our way throughout western Europe and made our way back to Amsterdam. We returned the van and caught the train to Luxembourg for our return flight.

In New York City, I met my high school friend, Jim Tramel. During my one year of high school in Nashville, Jim had been my best friend, loyal like a brother. When I lost my starting job on the basketball team, he bolstered my confidence then, saying things like, "Everyone knows you're better than the football guy the coach has put in ahead of you."

We had a loose plan to spend a few days in the city, wind our way through New England for several weeks, and then land in Kennebunkport, Maine. We had a tip from a college friend that a quaint hotel there would need new help near the end of the summer as staff started leaving. Sports again held a place in this part of my travels. One of our first stops in New York was the "old" Madison Square Garden, where we were able to walk about freely for some reason. Security then was minimal. Another highlight of these whirlwind few days in the city was a night listening to folk singer Tom Paxton at the famous Bitter End bar and nightclub that helped launch Bob Dylan and Joan Baez to fame.

The next day, we caught a bus to New Canaan, Connecticut, to pick up my red VW beetle at my great uncle's house. Then we headed to Cooperstown, New York, for the Hall of Fame baseball game. Jim had a good plan, in general, but with no internet to confirm the details, we got there just as the old-timers' game was ending. Our consolation was to walk around the field; no one held us back. We grabbed something to eat and came back to the modest little ballpark. To save money and savor the experience a little more, we slept in the bleachers, next to the third-base line. We did not see legends of the Major Leagues; we did drift off that night with the smell of mustard and stale beer in the air.

On our way to Maine, Jim guided us to the Newport Folk Festival, where we saw Arlo Guthrie sing a short version of Alice's Restaurant. That night, we folded the back seat down and slept in the red VW, freezing on a very chilly July night in Rhode Island. Then we met some of Jim's friends in Somerville, Massachusetts, a suburb of Boston. After travels through Europe and New York, I began to feel a bit lost, which Jim could sense. He found us a gym at Tufts University, and we shot baskets for more than an hour – vigorous one-on-one and H-O-R-S-E games. Endorphins shooting through my system again, with the combination of exercise and competition, I was ready for the last leg.

The four weeks in Kennebunkport were a perfect ending to a jam-packed summer, which welcomed me into a vast world. From canals in Venice and grass courts in Bristol, from bleachers in Cooperstown to the freezing waters on the rocky coast of Maine, I was no longer a sheltered southern boy. And I no longer felt protected from the impact of societal upheaval, as I had as a child in the safety of my family. The Democratic Party convention in Chicago at the end of August following the assassinations of Martin Luther King and Bobby Kennedy had put an exclamation point on a country at war with itself. And the real war for many young American men in Vietnam was turning sour in more and more stomachs, including my own. That summer of 1968, I was one of those awakening to the world around me.

19

Senior Year

Before going back to Duke for my senior year, I had a few days in Nashville to visit with my parents and sister. My hair was longer than ever. I even donned a thin chain necklace complete with a dangling peace sign. My 1967-68 annual college yearbook, the *Chanticleer*, was lying about. The opening words in the heavy tome got my attention:

A time of knowing is upon you.
It is up to you to discover yourself.
There are no other prophets.

About to begin my last go-around at Duke, the yearbook reflected my state of mind. "No one is immutable in this university situation," the introductory essay read, no one shall "escape unchanged." Whether "awakened or whether their existences remain pre-natal," students are surrounded by such possibilities as "an immoral, decadent America." And, white students specifically face the possibility of "continuing complicity in a heritage that threatens to make their own lives a dirty heirloom."

The essay noted possibilities that have surrounded my young adult consciousness: the destruction of cities, the possibility of America being wrong, the possibility of some students being more concerned with a demonstration at the

Pentagon than with Homecoming Weekend. And, too, it reminded us of the draft. "The world comes to the campus."

Wow. I had a lot to think about on my drive across Tennessee and North Carolina, back to the Duke campus. Those *possibilities* seemed like hard forehands coming at me in a long rally, driving me to my limit in a three-hour tennis match. How would I embark on the road ahead? And what role would tennis play, if any, as I ended this springboard of college into the world?

The fall of my senior year, I slowly began to take more steps towards adulthood. I ran for president of the fraternity, thinking we needed to spend some of our dues supporting poor areas of Durham, not just on bands and beer for parties. After winning, I did think about a more mature way, in my view, of spending our fraternity budget. But I lacked the experience or energy to garner support for what would have been a bold new step. I went with the flow, leaving the budget as it had been in the past, and turned my energy instead to my courses.

The world beyond Duke's gothic towers loomed on the horizon, but I had several more shots at these intellectually engaging opportunities that helped me think critically, linking ideas with the world around me. In American literature, where I enjoyed the challenge of writing essays three years after my freshman English debacle, I understood how themes in *Moby Dick* related to the human psyche. In American history, I read books like *Soul on Ice*, starting slowly to see the world through the eyes of a black man. And probably my best course at Duke came with professors from sociology, religion, and history joining together for interdisciplinary studies on India.

One day in the India class, a religion professor discussed the essence of soul and matter. No ordinary lecturer, he took us on a journey, like a guided imagery exercise, into the nature of life at the molecular level. By the end, I could practically *see* the individual molecules in my desk – or so this object *seemed* to be a desk. These atoms moved about in millions of tiny patterns even as we sat on these objects that somehow did not float into the air. The class time ended, but every student sat as if frozen by some spell. Finally, after 5, 10, maybe 15 minutes, we heard students banging on the door, waiting to come in for the next class. Still, no one moved. Finally, the interdisciplinary India assemblage began to shake the magic from our transfixed bodies and slowly stand. We made our way out the single door without a word, past the waiting students. My tuition for four years was worth that single class. Thank you, Mom and Dad.

By now, in this final fall semester, my feet followed the well-worn path from my fraternity section across the street to the gym in a more familiar kind of trance. When in doubt about how to spend a few hours after homework or to counter moods of despondency, my instincts led me to the gym. Basketball seemed even more engaging by my senior year, so much fun that year.

One evening, I went to the adjacent fraternity section to Tom's room. I trusted my doubles partner. "I'm thinking of leaving the team this year," I told him. "I'm better at basketball than tennis now. I keep getting better in basketball but kept losing last year in tennis. I'm tired of the grind in the second semester."

Tom agreed that our junior year had been a rough season, especially the finale: a terrible performance at the ACC tournament in Maryland followed by the disastrous 100-yard dash. But he reminded me that we had recovered during the trip to Europe. We regained some self-respect by stepping onto a grass court with some of the world's best players and solidified our friendship as we gallivanted across the continent.

"I'm a bit burned out by tennis myself," Tom admitted. "And as you know, I love basketball and miss being on a team. But come on Fingo, you're way better in tennis compared to basketball."

"What do you mean?"

"Think about it," Tom continued. "You're one of the best six tennis players in the school, right? But basketball. What, maybe one of the best 100 or more players – and that's not counting our varsity team. It doesn't make sense to quit tennis."

We continued to talk about how much we love basketball compared to the daily practice sessions and losses on the courts. Finally, Tom came up with an idea.

"How about playing in a city basketball league? We can get some of the guys from your intramural league team that did so well last year. We'll have tough competition, regular games, and a chance for a trophy if we win the season."

I agreed to stay on the tennis team if Tom would play on our city-league basketball team. We went back to our routines, studying to make sure we did well in our final year, to graduate and move out into the world with confidence. The city league began before Christmas break and ran through the first part of winter and early spring. Just as tennis practice started for our last season, we wrapped up the city basketball league. Against taller and older teams, some with players who had competed on college teams, we won the championship. Tom still has the trophy in his attic.

My Last Season

Now at my 50th college reunion, I leave the modern new student union building, closing my reflections at the exhibit of published books. I am proud of completing and publishing *The Crane Dance* and having it included in this class reunion. Walking past the old student union, heading towards the tennis courts again, my mind turns back to that last semester and my last tennis season. My feet seem to find familiar spots in the worn cobble-stoned paths through the dormitory and fraternity quadrangles. So many years have passed, so much change. So much to be grateful for.

My last year of tennis starts to come to mind. Tennis began as usual that winter of 1969, with skin cracking on my right thumb and forefinger, dry from long practices on cold February days. We donned nondescript sweatpants and shirts that the Duke athletic department allowed us to check out with "Duke PE" printed on the gray fabric, no "Duke tennis" logo. The minor sports were still bare-bones operations my last year. We did have a set of lockers in a room off the main student locker room, and I knew we would go to Florida again for spring break. I found the predictable surroundings and schedules ahead a comforting reminder of my cozy life on a college campus with no real responsibilities. All of this would end in a few months.

That year, I knew I had a spot somewhere on the team, between number 3 and 6 tier for singles, so challenge matches were not stressful. However, a shift in doubles did add a twist. The coach put Tom and Don ("Bernie") together, leaving me with a new partner my senior year. In early March, when our first match arrived, I missed Tom, my doubles partner for the last two years. But two other new elements to the season far overshadowed the doubles issue.

The third week of March, we had four easy wins at home before heading south for our annual trip during spring vacation. First stop: Clemson, one of the buzzsaw teams of the conference. The Clemson Tigers tamed our forehands and backhands as if we were purring kittens. We put our tails between our legs after the 9-0 whipping and headed south to Florida.

On that long drive, I did not think about the pretty college girls we would see on the beach. My mind kept turning instead to a pretty girl back at Duke. I wondered if Georgia might come to see my matches when we returned to campus. Another preoccupation traveled with me to Florida – where would I go after graduation?

Georgia and I had discovered each other in February in a fourth-period class, Religion and Contemporary Literature. She was a religion major; I was checking out interesting classes in my last semester. Over the decades that followed, as Georgia and I would tell the story of how we met, she always would lead with the size of my feet. In class, I often placed my size-11 shoes on the edge of the bench in front of me, where she usually sat. We sat in desk-like sections of benches, with a fold-down writing surface at our disposal for taking notes.

My version of meeting, however, is through my stomach. In the 1960s, all the women's residence halls (except for nursing students) were on East Campus. In the women's dining hall, you paid a flat fee for all you could eat. Men usually ate on the main West Campus near our dorms, where the dining hall charged by the item, a la carte. At the end of our midday fourth-period class, which was on East Campus, I walked toward the dining hall, where I could eat all I wanted for a flat fee.

There we went, a pimply, lanky guy with a large athletic stride atop big feet amidst a group that included this smiling face framed by long dark hair. Neither of us can quite nail down how we began to separate ourselves from the others. But we both remember our conversations at lunch lasting longer and longer, other classmates long gone. The stories we told never seemed to run on and on or lack engaging twists and turns. Listening was not an effort, but rather a tonic. We seemed to be walking down parallel tracks that somehow seemed part of a single unfolding story, even then.

I had two lives growing up, in Mississippi and those summers at Lake Junaluska. Her two lives were in Illinois and in Washington, D.C., where she would go each year when her father's government job took him to the nation's capital. We both were fascinated by spiritual questions, not from church backgrounds but from some common, inherent curiosity. And, she was drawn to service, volunteering in a nursing home as a college student. She told me about her trip with a group assisting with education and medical care in a coastal Nicaraguan village the summer before.

I told her the type of service I was considering upon graduation. Should I go abroad as a Peace Corps Volunteer or stay home and work with VISTA, part of the new federal War on Poverty? John Kennedy's famous words rang in my ears as the last semester began: "Ask not what your country can do for you, but what you can do for your country." Would I try for the Peace Corps, following a travel bug that the summer in Europe sparked, or would I look for a VISTA position in Appalachia to be part of those North Carolina mountains where I had spent so many wonderful summers? I was gradually shifting to a life of actual service, not just thinking about the importance of service. After the assassination of Dr. King, the 1968 Vigil had begun to wake me up. With my protected life at college about to end, I felt the need to step into action.

During the rugged February practices, I decided to put on some muscle. Maybe meeting Georgia motivated me to fill out my skinny frame. Or maybe I was determined to be the best athlete I could be in my last semester of competition. I lifted weights regularly, adding some definition to my taut but thin arms. This was my first time lifting weights since around age 12, when little Mike Jordan and I lifted light weights in the summers at Lake Junaluska. Mike eventually won the ACC wrestling championship in his weight category. These workouts made me stay longer for more calories at the East Campus dining hall. And to linger in the enthralling conversation and the eyes and spirit of this woman, Georgia.

New Factors

On the Florida trip, after the Clemson whitewash, we played a weak Florida Southern team in Lakeland, Florida, where my brother's girlfriend was a senior. My brother was on spring break from graduate school and came to the match. He had introduced me to tennis as a kid and kept up with my tennis career. He had also seen a few of my matches my sophomore year when he was in a master's program at Duke. He still remembers my doubles win against Miami my sophomore year, as well as my win that day on a picturesque Florida Southern campus.

On the ride home from our Florida week, I was entranced with an article about the eccentric Danish world class player, Torben Ulrich. He talked about body awareness, including how he noticed each nuance in his feet as he walked up a flight of stairs and the fact that he viewed sports competition as a western version of yoga.

"You talked about Ulrich all the way up the East coast," Tom says in one of our recent phone conversations. "Then we got to the South Carolina match – and you got killed!" Tom laughs at the memory, sharing stories more than 50 years after that match. His infectious, spontaneous cackle still makes me smile. I laugh too, remembering my fascination with Ulrich. Body awareness, including yoga, did become an important part of my journey, as well as the realization that such awareness alone cannot win tennis matches against much better players.

After we returned from Florida, we added to our early season success with six straight wins, taking our record to 12-3. But we knew what was ahead, our final four matches against strong conference teams before the ACC tournament.

While I played hard and certainly wanted to win, my mind would often turn to Georgia. During matches, I would glance over to see if she noticed my good shots but then tried to hide in the exposed open court when I missed an easy volley or netted a forehand. Having Georgia at the matches after spring break made the outcome less important than previous seasons. No more storming off the court after a close loss, as I did several times in my sophomore and junior years. Now, win or lose, I would find a towel and orange slices and quickly head over for a quick conversation before Georgia had to rush back to East Campus.

A second big preoccupation during matches was my future. Recruiters came to the campus during the winter and spring, trying to entice graduating seniors to a new career. Of the handful of business majors in the economics department, I was the only one who did not sign up for multiple interviews with large companies. Instead, I visited the Peace Corps and VISTA recruiters. The lure of travel proved strong, as had a friendly Peace Corps recruiter who found a good assignment for me in Tunisia, where my French would help.

Late in the spring semester, I got a letter telling me the Tunisia spot was no longer available. Due to political unrest, the Peace Corps had to pull out of the country. I felt a wave of panic, realizing that I would probably be drafted and go to Vietnam. That was a route I was not willing to take, but what could I do? Near the end of the tennis season, the Peace Corps wrote again, saying they had found me a spot, in the marketing section of an Indian poultry project. My economics/business major helped at last, as did my India interdisciplinary course. I felt ready and excited.

Reunion Reminiscing

Before my 50th reunion, I researched the Duke University archives to see what records existed on the tennis teams for 1967, 1968, and 1969. Short Associated Press articles covered our home matches, and summary sheets from the sports information office included our schedule and team results. I also exchanged several long emails with Tom and learned he had a clear memory of several of our doubles matches. We talked on the phone about his memories, sadly missing any reflections that Don and Chuck may have shared.

Reading the scores from my last ACC tournament, 50 years later, I feel proud, even though I lost more than I won. I do not remember match details such as a key double fault or a timely winner. The scores from the news clippings do, however, remind me of the subtlety and nuance of the game that I am discovering again in my 70s. I can feel the excitement as players gather at the opening of a tournament, the thrill of winning a close match and the disappointment of a long three-set loss. And, from recent tournaments in my 70s, I know the bounce I must have felt at my last ACC tournament, held in 1969 at nearby NC State University in Raleigh. As players gathered, I joined in, part of a tribe.

In the first round, I lost a tough three-setter in the No. 6 singles flight. Then, later that day, my partner and I lost at the No. 2 doubles flight to mighty Clemson in a close match, including a 10-8 score in the first set. Heartbreaking but nothing to be ashamed about. After the two close losses against very strong players, I drove my little VW bug back to Durham. I surely replayed some close points that might have turned the tide enough for an upset win. But I knew I had done my best.

Now in the losers' quadrant, I had two matches left, in singles and in doubles, to determine where I would finish, anywhere from fifth to eighth in my last college tournament. There was plenty of work left to do. The second day, I beat the NC State player in singles and, with my partner, eased by a strong South Carolina team. On the final day of the weekend tournament, my last day as a Duke tennis player, I played for fifth or sixth place. In these final college matches against strong players, I lost. I walked off the courts with a sixth-place finish in both singles and doubles. Overall, Duke finished seventh in the tournament.

The clippings did not tell me the most exciting moment of the tournament for the Duke team, and for Tom, the most memorable moment of his entire college tennis career. Late Sunday, Tom and Don were in a long third set in the Number 3 doubles flight, fighting for third place in the conference against UNC – the perennial archrival of Duke in all sports.

"Everyone on our team had gone home," Tom remembers. "Everyone at the tournament had gone home except for the Clemson and North Carolina teams and Dr. Bonk. If we won the match, Clemson won the tournament, and if Carolina won the match, they won the tournament."

By this time, after four years of engineering, three years as roommates, and now a season of doubles, Tom and Don were like brothers on the court. Tom remembers. "We played great, anticipating where the ball was going. Bernie was fabulous. And I hit great too, my injury out of mind."

The teams split the first two sets 6-4 for Duke, then 6-4 for UNC. The third set went to 4-4, then 5-5, 6-6, 7-7. In 1969, you had to win by two, no tiebreaker yet. Finally, Tom and Don edged ahead at 8-7 and won the final game, a 9-7 win.

"It was my only varsity victory over North Carolina in three years," Tom says. In fact, in our three years of varsity tennis, Duke University had never won any match against UNC, singles or doubles. Several weeks later, we went through our final exams. I took a trip to the beach with buddies between my last exam and graduation. I found myself reading a novel rather than drinking beer or getting sunburned on the beach. Maybe those "possibilities" in all caps in the *Chanticleer* were clicking in, just in time before I headed into the world.

I also thought about how much I would miss tennis. The Peace Corps in a place as challenging as India would be a bold new world for me. Tennis had played the role that nothing else could quite do for me in college.

It gave me a home with a small band of brothers, a tribe that took everything we could give on cold February practices and burning hot matches in May. I knew when I left Duke that the sport I discovered as a kid in Jackson was now deep in my life, even my soul. It provided a guiding light that I might need down the road.

After graduation, I drove my little VW to Chevy Chase, Maryland, where I met Georgia's parents for the first time. Over the next seven years, I would be in and out of Chevy Chase, finally standing beside Georgia in 1976 to say, "I do."

Part IV

Bill Finger (left) and Ken Gillespie, doubles partner at the
2019 NC Senior Men's Tennis Tournament

● 20 ●

Siren Song:
State Championships

The 2019 North Carolina Senior Men's Tennis Tournament calls me like a siren song. I have been to Jackson to revisit my early years with tennis and to Duke to replay my college years. Now I have a chance at age 72 to remember the third major period of my tennis career, my young adult years.

As I make the last turn indicated by my phone GPS, I wonder if I put in the wrong address. The narrow road, with a few houses nestled down on the left, seems more like a drive into a state park than a busy upscale section of Charlotte, NC. Slowing under the tree canopy, I barely have room to pass the car heading towards me. Still no indication that the largest and most prestigious tennis club in the state lies just ahead. Built in 1962 near the prosperous Myers Park area of then still sleepy Charlotte, Olde Providence Racquet Club emerges beyond a small sign to my left.

I park and stretch after the two-and-a-half-hour drive from my home in Raleigh. Walking toward the two-story clubhouse, I feel confused again. This is an entirely different view than my memories of the 35-and-over tournaments at Olde Providence when I played decades ago.

The entryway, parking lot, and now a modern, two-story structure – all new to me. A large porch on the second floor offers a view over three banks of green Har-Tru clay courts. I walk down the steps where I see the registration area under the porch overhang, shielded from the mid-day sun. At the bottom, close to the courts, I take a deep breath, happy to be at Olde Providence again. The empty courts look like a giant easel awaiting the arrival of the artists. Hot, tennis-ready air hangs over me.

A nagging discordance with the club layout fades before my gathering thoughts. This weekend, I want to win more matches in the 70-and-over division than in my middle age attempts. The word *SUCCESS* flashes neon across my mental screen. I breathe it in and chuckle, noticing some edits to my thoughts: *I've already succeeded. I'm here, competing, at age 72.*

A few other players are arriving. We nod, acknowledging the fraternity that gathers before doing battle. I look across the courts, my home away from home. New thoughts: *No worries in Raleigh. My wife is happy to let me go for a few days. No children at home. No deadlines in retirement. No injuries. No pressure. Just have fun. Do my best. And, oh yes, win!*

After I get my meal ticket and dark blue tournament shirt, I schedule a practice court. Then my doubles partner walks up.

"Looks like we'll have time to warm up before our first matches," I tell Ken Gillespie, who drove down separately from Raleigh. "I got us a practice court."

"Great. Let me get registered."

"I'll head down to the court," I say, pointing to the far area behind the main bank of courts. Matches in the various age categories, from the 30s to the 85s, will begin shortly.

These moments before a tournament begins have a mystical quality. The large swath of green clay looks and even smells pristine, like fresh dew from a farm field. The surface lies fallow, untarnished by footprints, by slide marks stretching for a shot, or from a dragged toe behind the service line. Long white borders provide order to these open spaces, with perpendicular service lines and baselines establishing the geometry awaiting to be tested. Mesh barriers with posts divide the space into identical twins providing an obstacle, a challenge. Opponents must find a way to send the ball over this division point, trusting the path will find the right mark on the other side, no longer in one's control.

Ken arrives at our practice court a few minutes after me. Our warmup gives us time to loosen our bodies and move into some full-throttle strokes. I bounce into a ready position for a volley, hit serves to the deuce and ad courts, and return Ken's serves. Warm-up time for a match in these U.S. Tennis Association-sanctioned tournaments is only five minutes, not enough time to work the body into performance mode.

My first opponent, Ted Pearce, still practices law in Charlotte. "He's a very nice guy," my Raleigh friend Keith told me a few days earlier after we saw the draw. "You shouldn't have any trouble with him."

At 6 feet 2 inches or so, Pearce has a long and lean body that could lead to a powerful game. Early in the match, I see that he will make too many errors to be a serious threat. Perhaps he has not had time from his law practice to sharpen his game. I am discovering that even as elder athletes we can change our body memory with practice, adding consistency to difficult shots. Such change takes time during the eighth decade of life. I know I need to be patient with myself, practicing serves over and over, trying to reduce double faults, a nagging problem since childhood.

As we put our rackets away after my win, Pearce chats about what he calls the highlight of his tennis career. "I played in Croatia last year," he says. "You know about the international tournament they had there?"

"Yes, I have a friend who's played in it. There's the team competition, where the players are selected to represent the USA. And then an open competition. Right?"

"Yep. Anyone can enter the open tournament, and I did. Played in a big stadium with an umpire. No fans though." He laughs. "Yeah, I'll always remember playing there." Walking back to the clubhouse, I wonder what moments I would identify as highlights of my tennis career.

Ken won his first round handily as well. His opponent, a college athlete who had taken up tennis late in life, had the competitive instincts and athleticism to push Ken. I was glad my doubles partner did not lose the close second set, which would mean he would have to play a third set. That scenario might tire him before our first-round doubles match later that afternoon.

First Doubles Match

Usually, the key to doubles is winning games when serving, known as "holding serve." Good returners can shift that advantage with sharp slice returns or clever lobs over the net man. Ken likes to hit lobs as serve returns from his deuce side, often landing them inches from the baseline. I like to slice backhand returns from the ad side or hit hard forehands at the opponent's feet if he rushes the net. While Ken and I have not played together in a tournament, we do sometimes play together at the Raleigh Racquet Club. Our skills mesh well.

Our first-round opponents, Terrell West and Charles Brock, have strong serves. Attacking them with lobs or slices proves difficult. They hold serve through their first three service games, but so do we. Then, ahead 4-3, with no breaks of serve, Ken's lobs fall near the baseline, giving us advantages at the net. And I connect on several hard forehands, giving us a break in service. We take a 5-3 lead and then hold serve to close out the first set at 6-3.

The second set is tighter, with neither team moving ahead more than a single game, until finally we are tied at 6-6. At that point, we play a tiebreaker, where the first team to seven points wins, or higher if needed to win by two points. They get an early advantage and hold it to win. We each have a set.

The third set will decide the match.

By now, our style of play has them off balance. I hit more power forehands and volley winners, while Ken uses off-speed volleys to complement his lobs. We break serve and take a 5-3 lead. Serving for the match, I make unforced errors on the first two points. We're down love-30. Then Ken misses twice. We lose my serve at love.

Now they are serving, back "on serve" as we say. They hold serve and even the score at 5-5, then break Ken's serve to take a 6-5 lead. Somehow, after losing three straight games, we manage to break back, taking us to 6-6 and a tiebreaker to decide the match.

In a flash of points, we are down quickly in the tiebreaker, 1-4. "Come on Ken, we can pull this out," I say. He nods. I see in his eyes that we are both focused, ready for the next shot and not looking back – one of the most important aspects of a tennis match. Neither of us is lingering on what might have been when we were ahead 5-3, serving for the match.

We hold our poise. They are serving with the 4-1 lead. We deliver two excellent serve returns and then make a good serve ourselves to tie the score at 4-4. Then we edge ahead and have a match point at 6-5. But they tie it at 6-6. We get a second match point. Tied again. Then a third match point, but still don't close it out. Finally, at our fourth match point, we win the tiebreaker, 9-7.

We throw our hands up and screech, "Yesssssssssssssssss!" Our opponents were good sportsmen throughout, including the handshakes at the net. But they can hardly speak after-wards, so stunned and disheartened. As Ken and I head to the clubhouse, tension gone, we relive the last few points. Then, at the official's table, we turned in our score: 6-3, 6-7, 7-6.

Ken and I mingle with several other players, accepting congratulations. Our opponents were understandably not eager for chit chat. But they have won and lost many tourna-ment matches over the years. Thirty-five years earlier, Terrell

West ranked seventh in North Carolina among the 61 players listed in the 35s division. "Tough loss," I say to West as he gathers his racket bag, about to leave. "Obviously, with it that close, it could've gone either way."

West pauses for a moment, then boils the match down. "Ken killed us with his lobs, and you hit so many volley winners."

Happy with the victory, I take off my tennis shoes and rest by the closest courts. Then I see Art Abbott, the top seed in the 70-and-over singles draw and a former pro at the Olde Providence Club. I have gotten to know him at a few tournaments in the last two years.

"Hi Art. I got a question for you."

"Sure, shoot."

"I can't figure out the layout here at the club. Are these the same courts we played on many years ago in the 35-and-over division?" I motion to the courts in front of us, now silent after a day of matches.

"No, the club went through a major overhaul when they built this new clubhouse. The old clubhouse and the main row of courts were behind the trees over there." He points to the distant area behind the back courts where Ken and I warmed up. "The club is a lot different now. The pros work with kids in a separate section."

"Aha. Now I get it. No wonder I couldn't quite get my bearings." With my confusion settled, I am ready to enjoy dinner.

Friendship Takes Unexpected Turn

Ken and I are happy to get advice from one of the club officials on an informal restaurant just a few blocks away. Tired from the long, close doubles match and the first round of singles earlier, we elect to go past the room with a live musician and head to a table in the back. The eclectic, well-known songs seep into our area, like those distant memories of Olde

Providence – Beatles tunes, classic country and western. After ordering, we talk more about our victory, smiling and laughing.

"How can you drop those lobs inches from the baseline," I say. "Amazing!"

"You saved us so many times, poaching on the net, saving my weak second serves," Ken replies.

After the food arrives, we focus on pasta, salad, and fish. No need to talk now. As we begin to slow down with our food, Ken looks up and asks a normal question between friends, now on our first road trip together. "You have kids, right?" In our doubles games over the last year or so at the Raleigh Racquet Club, bits of our lives away from tennis popped up at times. But we have never really talked about our families. "So how many?"

In recent years, I have answered that common question in various ways. A new dental hygienist asked the same question not long ago, chatty as she poked and scraped at my teeth. When she pulled back and raised her eyebrows, waiting for my answer, I said, "We have one daughter."

But tonight, I decide to share more of the story. "We had two, a son and a daughter. But our son died about six years ago." Ken looks up from his plate, serious. His usual quick wit and gregarious conversation take a sharp turn into silence. We both sit still, a cocoon-like bubble holding this raw information safely. Even the mellow sounds from the guitarist seem to stop at the edge of sorrow.

Feelings from nearly six years earlier, after my son's sudden death, bubble up. The intensity has subsided, gradually taking up less space in my heart. But the feelings remain, joining Ken and me at the table like an uninvited guest: shock, sadness, numbness, as well as gratitude for friends, support systems, resources, faith.

Books I pored over pop into my mind, along with sessions at the grief center with my wife at a local hospice organization, including support groups, writing sessions, and art programs. My wife and I took long meditative walks together along paths where our son liked to search for snakes and frogs in years past. So many conversations with close friends. Poems and blessings that took me beyond thought. A trip to the basement chapel of the Washington Cathedral with a mosaic of the resurrection, where I found myself on my knees, a strange posture, foreign to me since early childhood. As the years passed, my grief settled, not to be moved through or washed away but rather to be absorbed as part of my life experience and journey forward.

Silence hangs between us with a kind of respect and dignity, a stillness that seems better than words, like a kind visitor who joins our table with solace and support. The jubilant mood of victory has shifted from a replay of key points in our close win to a quiet teamwork of a very different kind. Ken sits as a comrade, allowing me space in silence.

We say goodnight in the parking lot, no hugs or lingering words, just checking that each of us knew where we were going. I put the address of my nearby Airbnb in my phone, and Ken heads to his motel. We confirm our times for Friday, singles and doubles.

Doubles is Like a Marriage

During my early 30s, tennis crept into the first years of my marriage. "Keep your wrist tight," I said to Georgia, standing on the grainy concrete court. Several large sand dunes separated us from the Atlantic Ocean. I had spotted the semi-abandoned court driving along picturesque Pawleys Island, South Carolina, where we had a week's rental at a little cottage. I had brought along a bag of tennis balls and rackets for the vacation, just in case. As we hit that afternoon, the salty ocean air invigorating us both, I noticed that Georgia could meet my strong forehands with her forehand volley without flinching.

"You're hitting a really good volley on that side," I said.

"Let's try these a little harder."

Georgia was and still is what sports fans call a "gamer." That day, with the salty smell of ocean waves drifting over the dunes, she flexed her knees a little more. She got in that ready position she learned in beginning tennis lessons as a kid and focused her steel-blue eyes on the ball in my hand. I knew this look well from many moments off the tennis court. I dreaded but oddly appreciated that ferocity when she had a problem with something I had done. At Pawleys Island, well past the courtship phase, we were still sorting out the team-work needed for a long marriage.

I bounced the ball and hit a hard forehand straight at her. *Boom*. Crisp volley return. "That's great! Well done!" I yelled above the sounds from the ocean. Her ability to hit such a volley, given her overall skill level, surprised me. Then I hit another ball, a little harder. When it hit her racket, she lost her grip as her wrist collapsed slightly, sending the ball into the net. "Good try. That was really a hard hit one. Keep the wrist tight."

Her eyes hardened. Knees bent a bit more. My next fore-hand raced through the ocean air, three inches over the net. Georgia adjusted her racket head slightly, wrist firm. *Boom*. Another winner.

The implicit bargain that week on one of the most secluded, picture-book getaways along the Carolina shoreline: she would hit tennis balls with me if I looked for shells with her. We each liked both activities, but she would have stopped hitting ten-nis shots long before my last formidable forehand. I worked hard at keeping alert to the subtle colors and shapes of the shells along the sand, and I even began to appreciate the pile of shapes accumulating at the back door of our cottage.

My wife had played a little tennis as a kid, and she was athletic, with competitive swimming and field hockey as the main sports in her youth. She had not kept up her tennis and now had a powder puff serve and a seriously limited backhand.

Even so, as we sorted out options for leisure time together as newlyweds, she was willing to get on the court with me. That week at the beach, Georgia gained a killer forehand volley, along with more confidence and interest in the game.

Back to our life in Raleigh, she began playing with a friend, Robin. They even entered the women's doubles in the 1979 Raleigh Parks and Recreation Department tennis tournament. She agreed to enter the mixed doubles division as well, our first tournament. We had two weapons: my overall quickness in covering the court and our secret, her forehand volley.

After an easy first round win against a weak team, we faced the fourth seed, our friends Bob and Patty Koury. Bob had won the state men's open championship a few years earlier and beat me handily when we played. Patty played about like Georgia, a beginner level game, but Bob had been working with her. She was improving fast.

In a tournament match, the goal is to win, not be polite. In mixed doubles, the winning strategy is usually to target the woman, even with hard shots. Bob's blister-hot forehand, sometimes too hard for me to handle, could take the racket literally out of Georgia's hand. We knew this going in, but had a plan.

Georgia played very close to one of the alleys, the strip of real estate down both sides of the court that expands the court boundaries for doubles. That left virtually the entire singles court and one alley for me to cover. Even so, early in the match, Bob hit his scary forehand right at Georgia. Georgia held her racket just above her waist, ready for a forehand volley, and *boom*. She blocked Koury's shot, ricocheting the power back to their court. A winner.

Bob shook his head. *How could Georgia do that*, he must have been wondering. He tried again, aiming for this small portion of the court with the tried-and-true strategy in mixed doubles – pick on the weaker player. Same result. *Boom*. Another point for us. As the match wore on, we had trouble winning

Georgia's serve, but even then, I was able to poach on Patty's soft serve returns and win some points. Bob never shifted his strategy, rarely moving his shots to open areas in the broad court I was trying to cover. He still picked on the weaker player, but Georgia kept responding fearlessly, usually with winners.

We squeezed by the Kourys in straight sets, on paper a match they should've won. After another close win in the next round, we drew the top seed in the semifinals. Using the same strategy, we won a close two-set match and then got the tournament trophy with a three-set win, 6-3, 1-6, 6-1. We were Raleigh city mixed doubles champions in our first tournament outing. The silver goblets with the 1979 date are still in our dining room china cabinet 40 years later.

In the women's doubles, Georgia and Robin had a close first round match. Robin was showing a distinct bump at about three months pregnant. Under a hot afternoon sun, I worried as they moved through a long third set. Even with Robin sweating and slowing down, they managed to pull out the win. The next day, though, they lost in the second round. After the tournament, Georgia and Robin still played together from time to time.

Some months after the tournament, Georgia suggested to Robin that she leave baby Charles with me while they played. Georgia wanted me to get a taste of parenthood. We had gone through a review with the Children's Home Society and were approved for adoption. One day soon we hoped to get the "happy call," as the agency referred to the one-day-notice to come pick up our new child.

One Saturday afternoon, Robin dropped little Charles off at our rambling old house in the Boylan Heights area near downtown Raleigh. "He'll be fine," she said as she put the four-month-old in the portable play pen. "He'll probably sleep. But in case he cries, here's a bottle and some blueberries."

As Georgia and Robin swatted forehands and backhands

at the nearby NC State University tennis courts, little Charles found his strange surroundings unnerving. I couldn't get him to stop crying. Only one thing helped – blueberries. I fed them one at a time. When crying returned, and my unskilled efforts at soothing him failed, I offered him another little round berry.

Game over and mother returned at last, Charles was happy again. When Robin changed his diaper, a parade of blueberries flowed out onto the changing pad. I must have looked as sheepish as I felt, but Robin and Georgia burst out laughing. No damage done to Charles, I surmised. I had survived my first-time home alone with a baby. Thank goodness blueberries were in season.

Georgia and I found ourselves in one other mixed doubles tournament the next spring, on vacation in Bermuda, kindly hosted by her parents. We saw the tournament advertised on a flyer from the parks department and told her parents. In their 70s, they agreed to play. When the day arrived late in our week vacation, stormy weather awaited us. We all decided to hope for the best and headed to the public court named on the flyer. Her parents arrived in a taxi while Georgia and I braved the sharp wind and cold on our rental scooters. The sturdy recreational department staff person, wrapped in a heavy coat against the stiff wind, watched us play an abbreviated match, three out of five games or so. We easily beat my new in-laws and won a sumptuous dinner for two at a local restaurant. But our mixed doubles career was mostly over.

About a year later, we got the happy call from the agency. Our first child came home in early 1981, a six-week-old bundle of "oh-my-god-what-do-we-do-now" joy.

At first, we still found a little time for tennis, playing with a couple who had a baby about the same time as ours. One day, we went to a local park with two usually deserted courts and put the two babies side-by-side in car seats next to one of the net posts. No screaming forehands that day. Only gentle shots that couldn't go awry toward the sleeping bundles of babyhood. But we never did that again. Naps got shorter and life

Courting: A Tennis Memoir

evolved. Gradually, between her job, the beginnings of a career shift, and our baby, Georgia drifted out of tennis. Between my part-time editing job, freelance writing, and parenting, I had less time for tennis but still managed to enter some local tournaments.

21

Humbled at Olde Providence

Friday morning at these 2019 State Championships in Charlotte, the clay courts again lie unadorned with footprints. No ball marks yet, not inside the white lines, half on the tape, or totally outside the boundary. These stately green lawns of clay sit waiting, ready to serve their purpose, to be enjoyed, fought upon, stumbled across, and raced through. This open space with mesh barriers and long straight boundaries includes water jugs, benches, and scoreboards. Meanwhile, at the club-house patio, players are gathering. Ken and I, along with others, are at the distant courts for a short warmup of bodies and strokes.

For Friday, the second day of action, the tournament director scheduled two rounds of singles for the 70-and-over division, along with a round of doubles. This would allow our division to be completed on Saturday. He was aware that the National Clay Court Championships for our age group would start this Sunday in Pinehurst, NC, and several of us in this tournament may be playing there on Sunday. Today in Charlotte, we have a long day of tennis ahead.

My next opponent, Charlton Lemon, a quiet, digni-fied player from Wilmington, is the only African American player in our division. The day before, he would have lost to his opponent, Scott Pollard, under normal circumstances. But Pollard, who has been ranked in various age divisions over the years, was coming off chemotherapy treatment. Tennis has been one of Pollard's anchors in life, and even with cancer and aggressive treatments, he wanted to be on the court. He took the first set from Charlton and led in the second before he stopped, conceding the match. Lemon moved to the round of eight to play me.

From a match with him in an earlier tournament, I knew Lemon hits a steady ball but lacks the pace needed to advance far at a state championship level. He also has a decent serve and the patience to keep the point going. My strategy is to be aggressive while avoiding too many unforced errors. I attack his short balls and move through the first set, losing my serve once, largely because of two double faults. Then he holds serve once in the second set, when I hit several unforced errors. I am happy with a 6-1, 6-1 victory so that I don't have to expend much energy with two matches still to go on Friday.

Ken, on the other hand, is laboring in a match with Ran Coble, the number two seed. Once a strong player, Coble has garnered enough points from recent tournaments to get the seed, but he has slowed down in his court coverage. Also, both he and Ken seem to be having injury problems. With my match over, I watch both Ken and Ran stretch when they change sides of the court every two games, taking much longer than a normal changeover.

"What's going on?" I ask Ken from behind the fence.

"I tweaked my hamstring. Trying to keep it loose."

Ken uses lobs in his singles strategy as well as doubles, forcing Coble to take balls deep behind the baseline or hustle toward the net and hit them as volleys, as the lobs drop. These choices are hard for Coble. Ken pulls out the first set in a tiebreaker and then coasts a bit in an easier second set. With Ken's victory and my win over Charlton, we both move to the semifinals, where we will play each other later that day.

As our match begins, I decide to be aggressive at times but mostly to drop behind the baseline and hit deep strokes back to keep the rallies going. From my regular matches with Ken in Raleigh, I know he can be a challenge if his lobs land near the baseline. I also avoid thinking about our friendship in the middle of the match. My approach to winning the match is to stay focused on every point.

My serve is finding the mark, and I return his lobs deep. I am aggressive often enough to keep him out of his rhythm, which means fewer deep lobs from him. My serve return is also consistent, minimizing "free" points for him. After taking the first set 6-1, I lead 4-1 in the second when he holds serve and then breaks to move to 4-3. He is serving again, trying to even the set. I need to break his serve to keep the lead.

Close this match out, I tell myself. *Be aggressive. Don't let him into this game.* My serve returns land deep in the court, where he cannot hit good lobs or drop shots. I move ahead to 5-3 and prepare to serve. I concentrate on mechanics – head up, good toss, first serve in. No double faults. Ken manages only weak returns, and I close the set at 6-3, getting the win. I am glad to reach the finals and very happy to avoid a third set. We both have more energy left for our doubles match later that afternoon.

The Thirty Fives: A Wimbledon Gale

Thirty-seven years have passed since my first match at Olde Providence in 1982, the year I turned 35. I was excited to enter this new age division in tournaments. Early in my 30s, I played Raleigh city tournaments and even won the city championship in singles and then in mixed doubles. But I had not explored broader venues. And, I learned about the 35-and-over division, where I would have a better chance at winning than against guys in their 20s.

Other ex-college and strong players had the same idea that I had: matches should be easier in "the 35s," as people referred to the age division. In my first tournament, on indoor courts in Asheville, I played well but lost decisively to a guy who had played at the University of Tennessee and then at Wimbledon. Closer to home in the spring, I lost to the former University of North Carolina coach, who had also played at Wimbledon. Also, I lost in the first round to several tough players who had been playing the 35s regularly.

While my first year in the 35-and-over group had been disappointing so far, I was hoping for a better outcome in the state tournament. Then I saw the draw sheet. After what should be an easy first round, I would face the top seed, Karl Combes. After the first-round win, I asked my buddy and doubles partner, Joe, if he could check out Combes.

"I found out that he played at Wimbledon and other international tournaments," Joe said. "He was part of the Australian group that came along in the footsteps of Laver and Newcombe." Why would a protégé of Rod Laver, the best tennis player of all time at that point – and some would argue, on par with now the consensus greatest three of all time: Federer, Nadal, and Djokovic – play in a state-level tournament? Maybe he was seeking some glory in a new age division, just like the rest of us. He never made it big like his Australian mentors. In my long-anticipated breakout year in a new division, for the third time, I drew an ex-Wimbledon opponent.

Throwing caution to the Wimbledon gale that had blown through my year, I decided to go big on my first and second serves and try to attack his serves. I won a few points on my serve. But attacking his serve proved to be an illusion. The hop on his second serve jumped well over shoulder height, familiar to touring pros but not to reborn college tennis players hitting the 35s. When we changed sides on the odd numbered games, I looked up at Joe in the small bleachers next to our court. My plea for advice and support met a befuddled look with the universal, "What can you do?" shrug.

This first year in statewide tournaments humbled me. At times I felt silly, thinking I would be able to jump into the winner's circle. Adjusting my life and schedule to playing tournaments out of town required some compromises. At home, life was busy with a toddler, a half-time editing job, and freelance writing. Trips to the tennis court were a welcome diversion. When I went to weekend tournaments, I usually took draft articles to edit between matches. Gradually, I found my footing. I won a few matches in smaller tournaments, enough at the end of 1982 to earn a ranking of 26 out of the 54 men rated in the 35-and-over category in North Carolina.

The next year, I did better in several tournaments around the state and was optimistic going back to Olde Providence in September for the state championships. I won several rounds without facing a seeded player, reaching deeper into the tournament. Then I played a career military guy from Fayetteville named Hight Redmond. Ranked number 14 the year before, he stood between me and a top 10 ranking for the year. We had long, contested points, with each of us pulling out a set. Before beginning the third set, we agreed to take the allotted 10-minute break. I sat and drank water and vowed to remain aggressive, going to the net whenever I could. To my amazement, Redmond went into the clubhouse and got a cup of coffee. He casually sipped coffee as he walked back to the court. Never had I heard that caffeine was a good way to replenish lost fluids. But it seemed to make him more focused.

In the third set, he attacked harder. I kept pace and had several chances to win games. But I missed too many shots, many of them unforced errors. His aggressive game worked better than mine and gradually wore me down. I knew I could – and should – have won the match. The loss triggered some primal reaction that I did not expect. After I got back to the locker room, I changed into dry clothes, said quick goodbyes to a few friends, and sped out of the parking lot back toward Raleigh. I probably should not have been driving. My anger was building now into a rage. I don't remember driving the first 30 miles or so, getting out of town, zooming north on I-85. But gradually, my anger turned to a memory of a similar reaction to a loss.

That day, driving back to Raleigh, I saw myself storming off the Duke courts after a match I should have won. After the Duke loss, I strode past the coach and my teammates with my head down without purpose or direction. I seemed to wake up to my surroundings near the distant football field, not remembering anything about the 10 minutes or so that had passed.

I had lost many matches before at Duke and many in my brief 35-and-over career as well. But this loss in Charlotte, like the Duke defeat, seemed to touch on a more primal nerve than just winning or losing. The losses triggered something deeper buried behind the anger and rage. Tennis was serving a purpose, alerting me to deeper psychological issues that needed attention, but I was not yet able to follow that path. In losing to Redmond, I lost a top 10 ranking in the state for the 35s. I did move up to number 17, 10 spots from the year before, but 10 spots below him. He landed number 7 in the state.

Driving back to Raleigh, I gradually calmed down before re-entering family life. I was too embarrassed to talk to my wife or other tennis players about my irrational reaction to the Charlotte loss. The emotional firestorm seemed beyond what sports psychologists deal with, even if I had known such a person. Back in a busy life, I pushed any concerns down and did not pursue the issue that seemed obvious: how to accept losses with more grace and to learn from them, in my tennis game and in my life.

End of the Thirty Fives

In 1985, at my fourth state tournament at Olde Providence, I had more confidence, better consistency, increased familiarity with opponents, and a cooler head. Our family was evolving well, and I had a steady job. I had lost some close matches and dealt with the disappointment better. But I still had a lot to learn from defeats.

On a nippy September morning, I zipped my green windbreaker before heading to a back court for a third-round match. I was thinking about how I would play William Poore, ranked number 2 in the state the previous year, behind Combes, the Australian. I had had a good tournament year, beating Bill Cole, ranked as high as Number 7 in previous years, before losing to Poore in a popular tournament in Asheville, NC. I knew Poore's silky smooth ground strokes lay between me and winning games, much less the match. My only hope would be to attack with approach shots and try to win the match at the net, avoiding long baseline rallies, which he would win.

In the first few games, my strategy worked. Whenever one of his strokes fell even close to the service line, I took a risk and hit a hard approach down the line, following it into the net. Mostly, I won the net points and managed to take a few games. But Poore remained unflustered. I needed some breaks and couldn't afford careless errors. On one shot, moving into a down-the-line forehand, my windbreaker flipped open and in a micro-second altered my arm motion. The fraction of a degree curved the ball wide by an inch, point and game lost. Poore respected my game and played hard. His consistent and hard ground strokes sailed my way, with little margin above the net. Over and again, he would hit a passing stroke as I rushed the net. Seeking an advantage in the point too soon proved to be my disadvantage. He won in straight sets.

Gracious in victory, he offered a useful tip as we shook hands.

"You've got to pick your chances to go to the net. Sometimes you were too aggressive." As we walked back to the club-house, I remembered his passing shots, slashing low over the net just out of my reach. I played well, but he was better and more experienced in knowing how to win. No internal fuming today; I did the best I could against a stronger player. I felt more mature as a person and as a tennis player than a few years before in that nasty reaction to my Redmond loss.

In the 1985 rankings, Poore shared the top spot with a former University of South Carolina Number 1 player, Bobby Heald. Former Wake Forest players came in at numbers 4 and 6. Bill Cole ranked number 7. Former Clemson player Art Abbott got the number 8 spot. I came in at number 10 that year, my highest ever. Terrell West, my first-round doubles opponent in 2019, ranked in the top 15. Now, he only plays doubles. Scott Pollard, coming off his chemotherapy treatment, played a solid first round in 2019, before he defaulted. In the 1985 rankings, he was just below West.

By 2019, on my return trip to Olde Providence, Bill Cole has an eye condition that caused him to quit tennis. Bobby Heald, after a career as a teaching pro, has terrible knees and can only play an occasional tournament in doubles. The Wake Forest players no longer play tournaments. Poore's once dom-inant game has faded with time; he passes on tournament competition.

In the mid-1980s, when I was fighting to make the quar-terfinals in the 35s, I did not pay attention to those old timers hobbling along in the 70s division. Now, here I am, hobbling towards a championship match in that old man's division and paying little attention to the small draw of players in the 35s division.

Tomorrow I will play in the finals of the 70-and-over divi-sion, squaring off against another Atlantic Coast Conference tennis player, Art Abbott. We have both raised families, sur-vived losses, and now enjoy life with grandchildren. We still practice our tennis game, hankering for another win, even a state championship. Here we are, the last two standing in our old man's bracket.

22

My Old Doubles Partner

On this hot Friday in September 2019, the long day of tennis continues. Before I can think about the singles finals to be held on Saturday, Ken Gillespie and I take the court for doubles. In our division, we play each of the other three teams in a round robin format, the approach used by tournaments with small numbers of entries. The modest draw is a byproduct of the USTA emphasis on team leagues rather than tournaments.

When Gillespie asked me if I wanted to play doubles at the state tournament, I said I would first have to call Dick Heidgerd to see if he wanted to play. All of us play at the Raleigh Racquet Club. Gillespie and Heidgerd have been members for decades. I joined only after I turned 70.

"I don't think so, Finger," Dick said when I reached him. "Go ahead and play with Gillespie." I wasn't surprised since Dick had been active in team tennis for years, not playing individual tournaments any longer.

Dick and I played together for three tournament years, when we got as high as the number 3 team in the state in the 35s. My last trip to Olde Providence with Dick was in 1986, when I was 39; it was my last tournament for more than 30 years. Over the decades, he would, on occasion, invite me to fill in for someone in a doubles game at the Racquet Club. I would play once or twice a year in casual games and hit pretty well, but never tried to sustain my game.

One morning, not long after my 70th birthday, I was getting out of my car at the O2 Fitness Center parking lot. The familiar bellow of a voice carried across three rows of cars.

"Finger, how the hell are you?" Dick liked to work with a personal trainer at O2 Fitness as well as play doubles at the Racquet Club.

I was going to the fitness center three or four days a week after our son had died, to fitness classes for seniors called "silver sneakers." I lifted light weights and did gentle stretches with old people, some into their 90s, using walkers. I was not playing any tennis or even jogging anymore. I weighed over 190, with a tight fit into 36-inch pants. These are large numbers for a guy who has always been lean, even wiry, and played college tennis at 165 pounds, at most.

Dick usually followed a gregarious greeting with good ole boy chatter, honed over the years with fellow lawyers and tennis buddies. But this morning in the parking lot, he broke character and stood before me as if to deliver a somber message. His tone went quiet and contemplative. "I finished your book."

"Thanks for sticking with it, Dick, it's a long book." I did not know he had seen it, out now about a year.

"How did I miss all that – the depression you described in *The Crane Dance*?" He said the title, I think, to emphasize the ground he was about to walk, a different kind of terrain compared to the boundaries of a tennis court. Rarely over the years had we ever gone across the line from sports talk to the world of emotions.

"I thought we had fun playing tennis," he added. His face looked stone serious, an unfamiliar mixture of hurt and confusion. An unusual moment of silence followed. I noticed his square jaw, jutted out, assertive, rugged, even ready for battle of some sort. "Whenever I got down, I played tennis and felt better."

He had more to say. "We never decided to stop playing. We

just never called each other."

"I know why we stopped," I said.

"We beat Calvin in that tournament," he continued, ignoring my comment.

"Yeah, it was at Hollow Rock in Durham." I rolled with his story.

"That was it. You would step over into the backhand court and hit that inside-out forehand." In the parking lot, he demonstrated how I hit what was, in fact, my best shot. He pulled his right arm back behind the shoulder, then opened the torso as he led with the elbow, pushing the racket head towards the far corner for the opponent's backhand, imagined today across the parking lot toward the door to the gym. He smiled, reliving the memory.

"My forehand was on fire that day," I said, plugging into the memory.

"We took home, I believe, our only victory as a team in a major tournament," Dick said. He paused. I could tell he was headed for some new angle. I settled on both feet in the parking lot, as if in a tennis "ready" position.

"Ran Coble and I were talking about you the other day. He said one day you walked out and had two left shoes on and still beat him." Dick's belly laugh echoed over the parked cars, his happy-go-lucky side as appealing today as it was in keeping me loose during tight points 30 years ago. "Ran says you could come out after not playing for a year and still beat him."

"No way I wore two left shoes. But I did always seem to have the let cords fall my way against Ran," I said. "The balls always seemed to trickle over the net for winners. He hated that."

Long after my retirement from competitive tennis at age 40, Ran and Dick both continued to work at their games – lessons, workshops, tournaments, team tennis. After a full shoulder replacement, after seven years of playing left-handed, he returned to his stronger right-handed game, playing on a

55-and-over team that almost made the nationals.

"My kids grew up playing tennis. Most of my friends are tennis players. I play with my wife every week. Tennis has been like life and death," he said. "Tennis kept the marriage together, kept the friends together, gave me a law practice."

I listened to Dick's stories about tennis, his passion for its role in his life. Then I went back to his question. "I know exactly when we quit playing tournaments," I said. We reached his car and I told him part of the answer. "Do you remember Georgia bringing our little girl to Hollow Rock to see us play? It was during that doubles match we won against Calvin."

Dick had a quizzical expression. I can almost see him trying to move from the image of us on the dark-green composition court on the edge of Durham to watching my wife walk up with a toddler. "No, not really."

"We had just adopted Dana; she was two and a half." On that 1986 summer day, Dana clung to Georgia's hand, as if to say, "Don't give me away again." Now, her foster years were over. We were there for her, forever. Dark hair framed this beautiful, shy little girl who seemed a bit shell-shocked. Then I turned back to my partner on the court, back to Dick. We went on to win.

"With Dana's arrival, we had a lot going on." He shifted his stance, absorbing this information. Then I ended the story: "I never really decided to quit playing tournaments. That's just the way things worked out."

In 1986, when Dana came into our family, life changed. With our first child, five years earlier, we had but one day's notice before bringing home a six-week-old infant; the process with two-and-a-half-year-old Dana unfolded more slowly. We visited Dana a few times with her social worker, including a trip to the park and to her last foster placement. We took her alone to a swimming pool, where she floated about with my wife and silently looked at us.

In July, on what we call her adoption day, she moved in,

carrying her little blue chair across our gravel driveway to the backdoor. She spoke mostly in those first weeks through dark eyes that seemed to hold a mixture of excitement and panic, somehow accepting these new adults as a safe place, but hesitant to release the easygoing playfulness of a toddler. Her eyes and matching hair, as black as a night sky, held a cavernous set of pre-verbal memories that would only slowly, if ever, unfold completely.

Around this time, I had a dream. Gradually, over the years, I realized this dream, too, somehow played its role in keeping me away from tournaments.

In the dream, I am alone on a court. No Dick Heidgerd around. No Bill Cole or William Poore. No motivation to get better or even play. I look around and see trees rising high at the back, behind the baseline. On the side near the gate, only tall, thick vegetation appears, vines climbing high above the fence. Turning in all directions, I see only trees and brambles, like a forest. I can barely see the surrounding fence. The court is being swallowed up.

Walking around the periphery, I see no way out. I am trapped. The tennis court has me locked in. Tennis has long been a loving family, a safe harbor, but now it is holding me back from a broader understanding of the world. No way to leave, no way to find myself in the larger world. This place of refuge, this room of my own, no longer serves the larger self. The dream tells me to find a way forward, beyond a space cramped with history and coping mechanisms. I need to break free and discover new thresholds.

A Long Day, More Doubles

Friday afternoon, after two singles matches each, Ken and I are ready for our second doubles match of the tournament. The director put us on an outside court, further from the clubhouse than the two main sets of six courts, but with a small

viewing platform for fans. Singles rounds from younger players took over the prime courts for the late afternoon crowd.
Our opponents, both members of Olde Providence, brought
some supporters with them. In fact, their fans set their folding
chairs at the edge of the court, just outside the fence, rather
than sitting in the viewing area about 50 feet away.

George Mauney and Kevin Soden had not played together
in a tournament before. Mauney played state tournaments at
his home club for many years. In the 35-and-over division,
Mauney ranked as high as 19 out of the 59 ranked in 1987.
Soden, on the other hand, only started playing tennis about a
decade ago. Still, as he moved easily up and back from the net,
I could see the ex-college athleticism. He starred on his college soccer, basketball, and baseball teams. An injury derailed
him from a professional baseball career, but not before he
kicked his way through an Olympic soccer tryout.

My doubles partner, Ken, beat Soden handily in the first
round of the singles draw, but doubles is a different set of
skills. We knew we would have a tight match, hopefully not as
long and difficult as our three-set win the day before.

The match begins with both sides holding serve. We have
close points, a lot of deuce games, and several break points
against us. But we hold. After they realize that I hit hard volleys, they aim more shots toward Ken. Our strategy is prepared for this: Ken often stays on the baseline and hits his
deep lobs, keeping them off balance. We pull ahead and take
the first set at 6-4, with one service break.

In the second set, Mauney and Soden settle into a more
confident approach of playing their own best shots. The
momentum swings back and forth; they get a break, then we
break back. The set marches along at 3-3, then 4-4 and 5-5.
The tension rises along with the score. At one point, Mauney
hits a weak baseline shot to me, and I move in, preparing to
crush a forehand down the line at Soden's feet. He sees my
aim, backs up and gets his racket ready. But despite his athleticism, he can't touch the ball as it zips by him in the alley.

"I knew it was coming," he says to Mauney.

"Nothing you could do," his partner replies. "Sorry, I set him up."

I turn to serve for the game in the ad court, smiling. Maybe we can close this out. With a lot of years of sports competition under their belts, they dig in. Their fans practically at our elbows hang on for the ride. After a couple of long, tough points, the locals supporting Mauney and Soden keep chatting, even as we begin the next point. After our opponents win it, I look over to them.

"Please, we can hear every word during these points!" The edge of irritation in my voice surprises me. While I don't sound like John McEnroe confronting an umpire, I do sound whiney in my complaint. I quickly add with a more social, local-club tone, "Of course, cheer your team between points. But you're awfully close to the court for conversation during the points."

Their fans get silent, maybe with a bit of irritation at me. But now only the thwops of balls against the taut strings crack the silence in the approaching dusk. Then, in the approaching dusk, I hear the insects growing louder from the nearby clump of woods. We need to wrap this up to avoid going under the lights.

We have a 6-5 lead in the second set but struggle to close the deal – they tie us, now six all. Time for a seven-point tie-breaker to decide the set. Last match, we had two straight tie-break sets. I am tired and really want to end this match with just one. The points are tight as we go back and forth, each person serving twice before the other team starts the next pair of points. The score inches up, 1-2 to 3-2, the serving team moving up two points. But we finally break through on one of their serves, and they never catch up. We win the tiebreak 7-5 and the match in two sets. No third set.

One more win tomorrow and we can be state champions.

Ken and I return to the same café with a predictable menu,

easy directions, and time to process our winning lobs and volleys. No surprises in the conversation tonight, just weary locker room talk on some of the tight points in the match. We eat quickly and head back to our respective lodgings. Fortunately, my upstairs area in the Airbnb has a nice bathtub. I soak in the hot water and feel my muscles relax after two singles and a doubles match. The warm water relaxes my mind as well. Thoughts drift along. Tomorrow will be a big day – a shot at two state championships. I smile.

23

Last Man Standing

Finals in the 70-and-over division: Abbott vs. Finger. No longer numbers 8 and 10 in the state rankings, as we were decades earlier. We are about to be number 1 and 2 in this old man's division. We have survived life as well as tennis. Abbott no longer teaches tennis but still takes part-time gigs as an umpire at college matches. We both still like to play tournaments.

Abbott has not been the pro at Olde Providence for many years, but he is still a member, lives nearby and sometimes rides his bicycle to the courts. He has a home court advantage, with friends in the crowd and greater comfort with the courts. But now into my third day here, I feel settled into the surroundings. Plus, no more than 20 or 25 people will watch our match; this is not the Atlantic Coast Conference tennis tournament, just a couple of old codgers knocking a ball around, trying to grab the state's top ranking. A bit of an ice cream sundae for old age.

At 10 a.m., we head out to the first court next to the clubhouse patio. The temperature has climbed to nearly 80, certainly not as sapping as a 95-degree day in August, but plenty warm for a demanding series of short sprints to track down wide forehands or backhands. Not to mention a drop shot. Art Abbott can hit them all. Wins from the last two days give me confidence and a sense of rhythm to my strokes. I feel at home on the court. Let the fun begin.

In the first two games, we test each other with conservative shot-making before gradually moving onto riskier, harder shots. We each hit winners with few unforced errors. We both hold serve, 1-1. Abbott plays a steady game, moving the ball from my forehand to backhand with smooth strokes but nothing overpowering. I know I can stay with him with patience and concentration. But I lapse on both accounts. On my second service game, I double fault and then slip in several unforced errors. Maybe I start thinking too much about this being the finals, the pressure to win!

More patience does not arrive, and suddenly, it seems, I am trailing 1-5, serving to stay in the set. As I gather the balls, I feel calmness seep into my body. I need to interrupt his momentum to keep this set from rushing to a quick ending. *One good serve*, I think. *Let's start there.* I follow one good serve with another and win my second game. Now Abbott leads 5-2 and is serving for the set.

On the changeover, as I sit sipping water, I remind myself of a basic strategy: keep the ball in play, wait before I attack. I vow to stick with this strategy, and I break his serve for the first time. Down 3-5 now. I hold serve again, moving the count to 4-5, three straight games won. Now the pressure is on Art to close the set. My serve returns have good depth, with plenty of safe distance from the sidelines. He pushes his first shot after my return long, seeming a bit flustered, and I move in to hit a winner down the line. I stick with my strategy of keeping the ball in play, and I tie the set at 5-5. I hold serve to go up 6-5 and break him for the third straight time. I win six games in a row to take the set 7-5.

With a lot of long points and deuces, the 12 games take more than an hour. I sit and drink more water, tired after the marathon set and three days of tennis. The temperature creeps up now close to 90 degrees. Only a wisp of a cloud drifts across the sky.

Whether I lose concentration or run out of steam under the hot midday sun, I don't know. But I do know that Abbott proceeds to do to me what I have just done to him – win six straight games. The only difference: he wins the first six. This set seems to be over in the blink of a service ace. Then, we sit again, neither of us asking for a 10-minute break before starting the third and deciding set. I put on a dry shirt and feel refreshed.

The third set begins like the first, both of us holding serve. We are pushing each other harder now, going for slightly more angles on our cross-court strokes. Neither of us makes many unforced errors. We stay on serve, moving up to 3-3.

It is my serve now. After several long points, Art pushes me far to my left, where I manage to dig out a low backhand and then all the way across the court to reach the forehand he sends back over. I hit a tough slice down the line as Art charges to the net. He makes a great backhand volley to win the point. Tired and not quite focused, I do not take enough time and double fault. He plays another solid point and takes the lead, 4-3.

His serve has pace and good placement but is not overwhelming. I hit back good deep returns, making it hard for him to win the point outright with his second shot. I work hard on each point and come close to breaking back. But Art has too much experience. He keeps me off balance just enough and holds serve, barely. I stay focused at 3-5 and hold serve to make it 4-5. But I cannot find an opening in his final service game. He keeps pressure on me with deep strokes, coming into the net to win a couple of points. As I shake his hand at the net, I feel exhausted but proud of my performance. Abbott is state champion, 5-7, 6-0, 6-4.

Take a Deep Breath

The match with Abbott lasts well over two hours, and the temperature reaches nearly 90 degrees by the time we shake hands around 12:30. Despite the many long points, with the mental and physical stress, I feel serene walking the few steps up to the patio where the volunteers record the match results.

"I can't believe I lost six games in a row and then won six in a row:" Art says as we walk together.

"I guess that's right now that I think about it. I couldn't quite get back even in that third set."

"It was a good match. I'm sure we'll have more battles in the future." And with Art's final words, we drift our own ways. I join Ken, who watched the whole match.

"You played great," Ken says. "You came close to breaking him back. Abbott is tough. He does not make many errors."

"I need something to eat," I say. "And to get off my feet. We'll have our doubles match soon enough." Ahead is the third match in our round robin format. We stand 2-0 after winning the first two rounds, with one team left to beat to become state champions in our division.

As Ken and I are thinking about lunch, John Myer, tournament director, is coming towards us.

"I got a call from the team you were scheduled to play this afternoon," Myer says. "One of them has an injury. They defaulted." He pauses before spelling out the bottom line. "So, no more matches for you. You've won the doubles title. Congratulations."

Ken and I look at each other as the news sinks in. We give a whoop and add some high fives to our big smiles. Well past age 70, we may be more reserved than victorious teenagers but still can exude old-man, spontaneous joy.

"Wow! Really! State champions!" My voice is louder than it should be this near the courts. "The tournament is really over – and we have won?!" My breathing starts to slow down, and I continue in a normal tone. "I feel like we cheated a little, backing in with a default."

"You won two tough matches," Myer says. "You earned it."

"It's true Finger," Ken says. "We earned it."

By the skin of our teeth, I am thinking, remembering the last tiebreaker the first day. It could have gone either way. But at least they never had a match point.

"It would have been a close match," I say to Myer. "Could've gone either way." Ken and I knew that the defaulting team beat Mauney and Sodin worse than we did, including a 6-0 whitewash in their second set.

"If we did play them and lost, three of the four teams would have had a 2-1 record," I say. "How would you figure out the winner?"

"I would just send the results into the computer. It makes the calculation – counts sets won, and if needed, games won."

"I'm sure glad it didn't come to that!"

"So am I," Myer says. "We have a clear winner. When you get a chance, come over to the scorer's table. I'll get the size jacket you want. The winners get a jacket. I'll show you the design. And I want to take your picture."

We walk across the patio, pick our sizes, and step out into the sun, posing for the photo. I am now part of the permanent record at Olde Providence. I have come a long way from my first time here in 1982. The Australian who had played at Wimbledon dispatched me like a stray piece of clay on the court that day 37 years ago.

Ken and I, still aglow, head back to the patio. "I'm going to take off," he says. "Need to get back home."

"Have a safe drive home. I'm going to get some lunch and rest some before I leave."

Tennis Kept Me Alive

For lunch, I find a spot on the second floor of the clubhouse with a view directly over the first court, where I can follow the doubles semifinal match in the 65-and-over group. Art Abbott is playing down to a younger age group and is battling with his partner against the top-ranked team. He chose not to play in the 70s division, which made the victory with Ken a lot easier. After his hard match with me, Art is at it again while I'm relaxed with a turkey sandwich and chips.

I am rooting for Art to get into the finals.

On one exciting point, the ball dashes from one racket to another, with all four players in the action. Finally, Art races for a drop volley near the fence post. He cannot get to the ball in time and runs past the fence post, almost to the opponents' side of the net, before he can stop.

"Great try. Thought you were going to hit it off the post," Abbott's opponent says with a friendly but sarcastic laugh. No one would try to hit a ball off the post, maybe around it in a rare circumstance, but not off it.

"Did you hear that?" I ask the guy sitting beside me, also intently watching the game. "When he wins the point, he seems to say something clever to the other team. But when he loses the point, he never says anything. He could've said 'good effort' if he really needed to say something. It seems like poor sportsmanship to me."

The guy next to me says, "Yeah, maybe so." Noncommittal. He seems to have a broader view of the match, probably knows the players. He looks across the courts again and then back at me.

"Hi, I'm Scott Pollard," he says.

"Oh. You played that first-round match with Charlton." Pollard only needed to win one more game but defaulted, before Charlton then moved on and played me. "I'm Bill Finger, lost to Art this morning. I guess that's why this guy is irritating me some. I'm rooting for Art."

"I saw part of your match with Art. Tough loss." No comment about the sarcastic comments from Art's opponent. I wonder whether to pursue with Pollard the reason he defaulted. We turn back to the match below. After several more points, Abbott's team loses the game. The teams move to the benches to sip water and rest before changing sides of the court.

I turn back to Pollard. "Art told me you were sick, that's why you defaulted."

"Yeah, I've had cancer for a while now," he says without any show of emotion.

"Oh, I'm so sorry."

"Thanks. It's been around for a while now, so I'm used to talking about it."

"So, you can still play tennis, even during treatments?"

"Well, the doctor says I should rest several days after the treatment, but I really wanted to play. Tennis has kept me alive over the last several years. That's the way I look at it."

"What do you mean – like kept your attitude positive, because you love tennis?"

"That's part of it. But more than that. Tennis has kept my body much stronger. Even though I get exhausted playing, my body seems to be able to fight the cancer better. It has more strength. I think playing tennis has given me extra years for sure. But who knows?"

The doubles match resumes. We stop talking and watch. I continue to eat my sandwich, starting to recover but also getting stiff from sitting still. I glance again toward Pollard and see that he looks pale but otherwise not identifiable as a person who had a chemo treatment two days ago. I think about how tennis can help people stay alive – whether a stronger body fighting off cancer or a stronger attitude toward old age in general.

I need to stretch my muscles before the two-and-a-half-hour drive back to Raleigh. "Scott, it was a real pleasure to meet you," I say. "I need to move my old body around a little. Good luck with everything."

"Thanks, Bill. Good luck with your next tournament."

24

Victory Lap

The route out of Olde Providence is familiar now. As I guide my Prius up I-85 on cruise control, I have plenty of time to reflect on winning and losing, playing after chemotherapy, the thrill and heartbreak of tournament tennis. Questions roll across my mind about success and failure, loss and re-birth, and new stages of life. *Losing a match. Losing a son. Who could compare them? We use the same word: loss.* My ride home feels like a long victory lap through my psyche. I have never been a state champion, at any stage of my life.

Two of the best players in the state did not compete in my singles division. The top-ranked player was injured; he beat me handily in a tournament earlier in the summer. The second-best player, also not there, beat me in straight sets in the 2018 state tournament held in Durham. Abbott was probably third best in the state in our age group, with me possibly fourth, depending on whether several other players played in any tournaments. I could think of my second-place finish in singles as better than it really was. But if I diminished the accomplishment in singles, our backdoor route to the doubles championship seemed even more of a magic trick.

But why am I questioning these finishes? We won them fair and square, paid our entry fee, got to the tournament, juggled family schedules, took care of aging bodies – and after all of that, kept the ball in play.

Tennis has been an anchor through childhood, college, and starting a family and career in my 30s. Tennis brought joy and a diversion from dark waters that flowed in at times of transition and stress. Even so, tennis could not alone guide me into a deeper understanding of life's most difficult times or provide a roadway to healing. When I lost my job in 1988, at age 41 with our kids aged four and seven, my anxiety about work and money pulled me into a period of depression. I knew I needed to understand this recurring theme in my life and develop tools beyond forehands and backhands.

Of the 105,000 words in *The Crane Dance: Taking Flight in Midlife*, my memoir where Dick Heidgerd first learned about my depression, the word *tennis* appears just 12 times. These are casual references to a shirt or shoes, the context of meeting my wife, and the fact that I could hit a ball over a net. Other words take center stage: *Prozac* (61 times), *meditation* (35 times), *therapy* (36 times), and *dance* (a whopping 235 times).

Tennis appears in a psychologically charged moment only once, on page 195. I described a dance workshop where I feel "like I'm walking across vast continents, with so much to explore and to see and feel." This combination of artistry and physicality led to "so many more ways to express myself than just ... playing tennis," I wrote.

Through my midlife years, I won a different kind of contest: a broader sense of self. I drew on my body's wisdom and other tools to arrive at new thresholds in life. Then, when I turned 70, I was ready to come back to tennis, and two years later, to the state tournament at Olde Providence.

Time passes, needs change, goals evolve. New visions emerge. The writer Wendell Berry speaks to this process in his poem, "There Is No Going Back":

More and more you have become
those lives and deaths
that have belonged to you....

And so you have become a sort of tree
standing over a grave.
Now more than ever you can be
generous toward each day…

There may be "no going back" to what I was, but even so, my journey did take me back to Olde Providence. Over the decades in between, I walked through many lives and deaths. In my 60s, past the midlife saga of *The Crane Dance* but before returning to tennis, the hardest deaths arrived: our son, especially, as well as my best friend from high school, my first doubles partner in the 35s, and each of my parents. And after all of that, I turned 70.

Now, in old age, I call on my reliable friend, tennis. I am grateful that my body manages, even embraces, the vigor required to glide and sometimes hobble about the court. The game warms my heart like the rising sun, and friendships abound through our common experience of racket, ball, wins and losses, frolic and fellowship. Within such comfort and joy, disappointing losses still challenge my serenity on and off the court. Embracing each moment on the court offers lessons on attitude and focus, graciousness to myself and opponents, in victory and defeat.

As I seek to stand as steadfast as a tree, over memories of loved ones and my own past lives, I seek generosity of spirit for my time on a tennis court and throughout my life. I seek generosity for those I love.

On my ride home to Raleigh, I keep coming back from my reflections on midlife to the tournament at hand. I have a doubles title with Ken and a runner-up trophy for singles. I am a healthy 72-year-old tennis player with power and finesse, an even temperament on and off the court, and a capacity to reflect on a match as it unfolds – to reflect on my life as it unfolds. In a practice game or a match, win or lose, I can remind myself to be grateful, to pay attention in each moment, to embrace the mysteries of each point and the unfolding of a game, a set, a match. This joy no longer needs to distract me from pain. Tennis is joy on its own terms.

Acknowledgments

For years, Dick Heidgerd encouraged me to join the Raleigh Racquet Club. When I did at age 70, after a 30-year pause from the game, Dick functioned as my informal sponsor among his many pals there. At the Raleigh Racquet Club, Tio Campanile, Ken Gillespie, Bill Mears, Keith Sipe, and Mike Stewart, along with Jimmy Washington from a nearby Durham club, have been particularly helpful practice partners, role models, and guides into the world of senior tournament tennis. All of them have read sections of the manuscript and made helpful comments, as have tennis friends John Grace and Carol Ann Vest.

The professional tennis staff at the Raleigh Racquet Club have supported the refinement of my game and maintained an interest in my journey through the senior tournaments, especially: Brent Bennett, Philip Faulkner, Carlos Garcia, and Paul Goode.

Tom Farquhar, my doubles partner during our Duke University tennis days, read the section on Duke and provided the same helpful support he always showed on the court.

To all these tennis players and others, I owe a great debt of thanks and appreciation. Their love of the game has an infectious quality, a validation of my own love to be on the court and to find words to express how this game has helped to shape my life.

In the early stages of remembering my tennis past, the wise writer Heather Sellers helped guide me with support and advice. Also, in the early stages, participants in a writing class I facilitated patiently listened as I wrote week after week of tennis memories and emotions; their enthusiasm for my stories helped carry this project along. As the chapters took shape, writer buddies helped me sharpen the book, reading drafts that gradually evolved into a manuscript. Thanks especially to Drew Bridges, Karen Matteson, and Jeannette Rogers, as well as Gale Buck, Christy Buck, and Lauren Bridges. Other friends have read sections and offered ongoing support and comments, including Ann Burwell, Betsy Finger, Ellis Finger, Dana Kimball, and Alice Weldon. My lifelong friend Bill Weldon read the entire manuscript and helped me avoid some embarrassing errors. Finally, Nathaniel Lee Hansen, my editor at Atmosphere Press, offered great suggestions that helped me streamline the final draft.

Throughout this journey, the tennis and the book, my wife Georgia Springer has stood with me, the best doubles partner for life that I could ever expect or hope for. Thanks to the lucky stars that guided us into the same class, where we met in my last semester of college.

About Atmosphere Press

Founded in 2015, Atmosphere Press was built on the principles of Honesty, Transparency, Professionalism, Kindness, and Making Your Book Awesome. As an ethical and author-friendly hybrid press, we stay true to that founding mission today.

If you're a reader, enter our giveaway for a free book here:

SCAN TO ENTER
BOOK GIVEAWAY

If you're a writer, submit your manuscript for consideration here:

SCAN TO SUBMIT
MANUSCRIPT

And always feel free to visit Atmosphere Press and our authors online at atmospherepress.com. See you there soon!

About the Author

WILLIAM (BILL) FINGER grew up in Jackson, Mississippi. After graduating from Duke University in 1969, he went to India as a Peace Corps Volunteer. In midlife, he completed a Masters in Social Work at the University of North Carolina at Chapel Hill. His first memoir, *The Crane Dance: Taking Flight in Midlife* (2016), was a finalist in the Next Generation Indie Book Awards. He has been editor of a public policy quarterly, a consultant at the N.C. Legislature, and for the last 24 years before retirement, a writer and communications manager at an international public health organization. Since 1977, he has lived with his wife in the Raleigh, North Carolina, area, where they raised their two children.